GOOD NEWS STUDIES

Volume 3

The Light Of All Nations

Essays On The Church
In New Testament Research

by

Daniel J. Harrington, S.J.

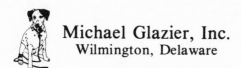

Michael Glazier, Inc.
Wilmington, Delaware

About the Author

DANIEL J. HARRINGTON, S.J. is professor of New Testament at Weston School of Theology in Cambridge, Massachusetts, and the editor of *New Testament Abstracts.* He is the author of *The Hebrew Fragments of Pseudo-Philo* (1974) *Pseudo-Philon: Les Antiquites Bibliques* (1976), *A Manual of Palestinian Aramaic Texts* (1978), *God's People in Christ* (1980), *Interpreting the New Testament, A Practical Guide* (1979), which is Volume 1 of the *New Testament Message* Series, and *Interpreting the Old Testament, A Practical Guide,* Volume 1 of the *Old Testament Message* Series.

First published in 1982 by Michael Glazier, Inc.
1723 Delaware Avenue, Wilmington, Delaware 19806
and Veritas Publications, 7-8 Lower Abbey Street, Dublin, Ireland

Library of Congress Catalog Card Number: 82-83682
International Standard Book Number:
  Good New Studies: 0-89453-290-1
  LIGHT OF ALL NATIONS: 0-89453-291-X

Printed in the United States of America
Typography by Peg McCormick

"Christ is the light of all Nations. Hence this most sacred Synod, which has been gathered in the Holy Spirit, eagerly desires to shed on all men that radiance of His which brightens the countenance of the Church. This it will do by proclaiming the gospel to every creature."

Vatican II's *Dogmatic Constitution on the Church (Lumen Gentium)*.

CONTENTS

Abbreviations in the Notes 9

Introduction 11

1. Ernst Käsemann on the Church
   in the New Testament 15

2. Baptism in the Holy Spirit 46

3. The "Early Catholic" Writings of the
   New Testament: The Church Adjusting
   to World History 61

4. New Testament Perspectives on the
   Ministry of the Word 79

5. Matthean Studies Since Joachim Rohde . 93

6. "Make Disciples of All the Gentiles"
   (Matthew 28:19) 110

7. Church and Ministry 124

8. God's People in Christ: Challenges for
   the Church Today 137

9. Sociological Concepts and the Early
   Church: A Decade of Research 148

10. The Reception of Walter Bauer's
    *Orthodoxy and Heresy in Earliest
    Christianity* During the Last Decade ... 162

7

11. The Ecumenical Importance of New
    Testament Research 174
12. Some New Voices in New Testament
    Interpretation 186
Index of Modern Authors 198

Abbreviations in the Notes

AB	Analecta Biblica
AGJU	Arbeiten zur Geschichte des antiken Juden-tums und des Urchristentums
ATR	*Anglican Theological Review*
BETL	Bibliotheca Ephemeridum Theologicarum Lovaniensium
BGBE	Beiträge zur Geschichte der biblischen Exegese
BHT	Beiträge zur historischen Theologie
Bib	*Biblica*
BTB	*Biblical Theology Bulletin*
BWANT	Beiträge zur Wissenschaft vom Alten and Neuen Testament
BZ	*Biblische Zeitschrift*
CBQ	*Catholic Biblical Quarterly*
ENTT	E. Käsemann, *Essays on New Testament Themes*
EvT	*Evangelische Theologie*
ExpT	*Expository Times*
FRLANT	Forschungen zur Religion und Literatur des Alten und Neuen Testaments
HeyJ	*Heythrop Journal*
HTR	*Harvard Theological Review*
JAAR	*Journal of the American Academy of Religion*
JBL	*Journal of Biblical Literature*
JES	*Journal of Ecumenical Studies*
JJS	*Journal of Jewish Studies*
JR	*Journal of Religion*
JTS	*Journal of Theological Studies*

NedThTs	*Nederlands theologisch tijdschrift*
NovT	*Novum Testamentum*
NTAbh	Neutestamentliche Abhandlungen
NTQT	E. Käsemann, *New Testament Questions of Today*
NTS	*New Testament Studies*
RelSRev	*Religious Studies Review*
SANT	Studien zum Alten und Neuen Testament
SBLDS	Society of Biblical Literature Dissertation Series
SBT	Studies in Biblical Theology
SJLA	Studies in Judaism in Late Antiquity
SNTSMS	Society for New Testament Studies Monograph Series
TDNT	*Theological Dictionary of the New Testament*
TS	*Theological Studies*
TU	Texte und Untersuchungen
TZ	*Theologische Zeitschrift*
VC	*Vigiliae Christianae*
WTJ	*Westminster Theological Journal*
WUNT	Wissenschaftliche Untersuchungen zum Neuen Testament
ZKT	*Zeitschrift für katholische Theologie*
ZNW	*Zeitschrift für neutestamentlichen Wissenschaft*
ZTK	*Zeitschrift für Theologie und Kirche*

INTRODUCTION

For more than ten years I have been the general editor of *New Testament Abstracts,* a scholarly periodical that every year provides brief summaries of about 1,200 articles and 600 books on the New Testament. During those years of abstracting and editing, I have from time to time written reports on various topics connected with the church in the New Testament. The issues that I have treated have generally been points at which scientific biblical scholarship and the life of the contemporary church intersect. The twelve essays reprinted in this volume illustrate how biblical scholars have worked in one area of research (the church in the New Testament) and furnish a record of some of the issues that have concerned the church and its people during recent years.

The essay on Ernst Käsemann's understanding of the church in the New Testament, which first appeared in *Heythrop Journal* 12 (1971) 246-57, 367-78, summarizes the views of an eminent German Protestant scholar and enters into dialogue with them. No one has stated the issues concerning the church in the New Testament as sharply and powerfully as Käsemann has, and few theologians have been as influential in both Protestant and Catholic circles.

The rise of the Catholic charismatic movement brought with it some questionable theology, and so the study on baptism in the Spirit published in *Chicago Studies* 11 (1972) 31-44 demonstrates the need to listen carefully to the biblical sources in order to appreciate the true nature of baptism.

One of the more unfortunate aspects of Käsemann's legacy has been the tendency to speak of "early catholicism" as if it were a single movement in the first century A.D. Close attention to the supposed sources for early catholicism in the New Testament reveals the existence of varied, though converging, responses to the crisis encountered when the church began to settle down in the world. The article first appeared in the *Festschrift* for F. L. Moriarty, S.J., *The Word in the World* (Cambridge, MA: Weston College Press, 1973) pp. 97-113. A very sound emphasis in Protestant biblical scholarship is the idea of the ministry of the word, and the appropriation of it in an official Roman Catholic document like the General Catechetical Directory constituted an encouraging development. My explanation of the New Testament foundations of this idea was published in *Chicago Studies* 13 (1974) 65-76.

Matthew's Gospel has long been known as the ecclesiastical Gospel, because of its concern with the church and its enormous influence on the life of the church throughout the centuries. The mid-1970's were a kind of magic moment in Matthean research in which Catholic and Protestant scholars joined forces to understand better the composition, life-setting, and theology of Matthew. My report on these discussions appeared in *Heythrop Journal* 16 (1975) 375-88. A special issue in Matthean studies was (and is) the Evangelist's attitudes toward Jews and Gentiles. Douglas Hare (a Presbyterian New Testament scholar at Pittsburgh Theological Seminary) and I treated this issue in *Catholic Biblical Quarterly* 37 (1975) 359-69. We concluded that Matthew was most eager to encourage his fellow Jewish Christians to undertake a mission to the Gentiles rather than to Jews.

An invitation to contribute an article on church and ministry in the New Testament to *The Pastoral Guide to the Bible* in *Chicago Studies* 17 (1978) 105-14 led me to synthesize in question-and-answer format the results of a decade of biblical-theological research. This was followed by a monograph on a key image of the church in the Bible—the people of God. I have included in this collection the concluding remarks (pp. 107-17) from my book *God's People in Christ: New Testament Perspectives on the Church and Judaism* (Copyright ©1980 by Fortress Press, reprinted by permission of Fortress Press).

In recent years there has been a growing interest among biblical scholars in terms and concepts developed in sociology. My survey, which was published in *Theological Studies* 41 (1980) 181-90, tried to express both the limitations and the possible contributions of the sociological approach to the study of the early church. While there is much value in the new approach, attention also had to be given to a classic in the study of the church in the first few centuries of its existence, Walter Bauer's *Orthodoxy and Heresy in Earliest Christianity*. The thesis of this book is that our traditional notions of orthodoxy and heresy are incorrect, and that more attention ought to be given to the local manifestations of Christianity in its earliest days. My article on Bauer's book appeared in *Harvard Theological Review* 73 (1980) 289-98.

The final two essays shift the focus from the early church to today's church. The one on the ecumenical importance of New Testament research, which was published in *Biblical Theology Bulletin* 12 (1982) 20-23, considers the role of biblical scholarship in promoting better understanding among the churches. The one published in *Anglican Theological Review* 64 (1982) 362-70, listens to the challenges presented to New Testament interpreters and to the church at large by third-world and other new voices in the International and interconfessional dialogue of New Testament research.

Daniel J. Harrington, S.J.
April 1982

1. ERNST KÄSEMANN ON THE CHURCH IN THE NEW TESTAMENT

If a scholar's achievement in any field can be measured by his abilities to determine the state of the questions in different research areas and to propose creative solutions which elicit learned responses from his colleagues, then Ernst Käsemann must be considered a major figure among New Testament specialists. On topics as diverse as the new quest for the historical Jesus, apocalypticism, the canon, unity and diversity in the NT churches, and "early catholicism" Käsemann's essays have been important turning-points in the recent history of research. Born in 1906, Käsemann studied briefly under Erik Peterson at Bonn and then with Rudolf Bultmann at Marburg and Adolph Schlatter at Tübingen. He served as a pastor for the Evangelical Church in the Rhineland and Westphalia from 1931 to 1945. After the war he returned to the academic world and has since held professorships at Mainz (1946-51), Göttingen (1951-59) and Tübingen (1959-71).

While Käsemann has written widely and provocatively on almost every aspect of NT study, a topic of special interest to him through the years has been the church in the New

Testament. From his first book *Leib und Leib Christi[1]* published in 1933 to his most recent works on freedom in the church[2] and on Paul,[3] Käsemann has returned again and again to the theme of the early church.[4] In this essay we propose first to explore Käsemann's contributions to our understanding of the church in the New Testament and then to examine in some detail the theological issues raised by this reconstruction.

General Statements

Among Käsemann's many writings on the early church, his article on unity and multiplicity in the NT doctrine of the church is as close to a programmatic statement as one might find and as such is a useful starting point for our own investigation. According to Käsemann the New Testament does not present an *ecclesiologia perennis* but merely offers certain ecclesiological archetypes.[5] Because there is an incessant process of change going on within NT ecclesiology, there are also corresponding changes occurring in eschatology, soteriology, anthropology and the doctrine of ministerial office.[6] Are these different NT "churches" united? At best Käsemann can only see some kind of ecumenical confederation without a real ecumenical council. In fact, the unity of

---

[1] *Leib und Leib Christi. Eine Untersuchung zur paulinischen Begrifflichkeit* (BHT 9; Tübingen: Mohr-Siebeck, 1933). This volume studies the concept of body in the Jewish and Greek worlds and in Paul and concludes with a discussion of the body of Christ.

[2] *Der Ruf der Freiheit* (Tübingen: Mohr-Siebeck, 1968); E.T. *Jesus Means Freedom* (Philadelphia: Fortress, 1969).

[3] *Paulinische Perspektiven* (Tübingen: Mohr-Siebeck, 1969).

[4] Two major collections of K's works in English are *Essays on New Testament Themes* (SBT 41; London, 1964) hereafter cited as *ENTT*; and *New Testament Questions of Today* (Philadelphia: Fortress, 1969) hereafter *NTQT*. See E. Osborn, "The Church in the New Testament. An Introduction to Käsemann's Account," *Colloquium* 3 (1970) 307-19.

[5] "Unity and Multiplicity in the New Testament Doctrine of the Church," *NTQT*, 252-59.

[6] *NTQT*, 255.

[7] *NTQT*, 256.

the church remains primarily an eschatological property, to be enjoyed only as a gift, never as an assured possession.[8] Käsemann sees a real danger in absolutizing the church. When the church makes itself the focal point of salvation and the theme of the gospel, when it pushes itself into the foreground so that Christ becomes a founder or a cultic hero, then it ceases to be the church of Christ.[9] In the true church of Christ the Lord remains sovereign over all his servants. The church gives the Lord's word free course and facilitates for the believer immediate passage into his presence. All tradition and all ministerial office within the church possess authority only as long and as far as they help to hear Christ addressing us; only the way of the cross can validate preaching. Finally, Käsemann observes that the worth of every ecclesiology is measured by the extent to which it succeeds in declaring the royal freedom and the lordship of Jesus Christ who, according to Eph 2, is himself alone the unity of his church.[10] This last element of freedom has been examined in more detail in Käsemann's recent book *Jesus Means Freedom*. So important and essential does Käsemann understand this mark of the church to be that he asks: Can a church or denomination call itself Christian if its devout members have ceased to be liberal and its liberal members ceased to be devout?[11] Jesus' own revelation, his glory, gift and claim is the message that God's children who were lost have now been reconciled and recalled.[12] When the church makes itself absolute and avoids the judgment of the crucified Lord, as it does in the "early catholicism" of the Pastorals, Luke-Acts and Ephesians, the word "freedom" becomes inappropriate.[13]

One cannot really understand Käsemann's notion of the early church without also exploring his views on the canon

[8] *NTQT*, 257.
[9] *Jesus Means Freedom*, 90.
[10] *NTQT*, 258-259.
[11] *Jesus Means Freedom*, 20. This book was written as a response to the attacks of the Fundamentalist *Kein anderes Evangelium* movement.
[12] *Jesus*, 41.
[13] *Jesus*, 85.

of Scripture. On the basis of historical considerations Käsemann adopts a rather critical stance toward accepting the
canon as the standard of Christian faith. The biblical materials speak directly only to the men of their own times; there
has been a process of selection and elimination of ideas and
movements; the canon as a whole is the product of "early
catholicism";[14] the canon itself presents four Gospels which
exhibit important divergences in order, selection and presentation.[15] Käsemann rejects as pure wish-fulfillment and
fantasy the notion of one biblical theology growing from a
single root and maintaining itself in unbroken continuity
and development.[16] Thus he is led to maintain that the canon
is not the foundation of church unity but rather the source
of diversity among churches.[17] By witnessing that many different confessions were already in existence, constantly
replacing each other and combining with each other and
undergoing mutual delimitation,[18] the canon itself provided
the basis for the multiplicity of Christian confessions.

The acceptance of John into the church's canon (which
Käsemann attributes to man's error and God's providence)
represents an intriguing case in point. Doctrinally this Gospel must be placed on the trajectory which led from the
enthusiasm of Corinth and 2 Tim 2:18 ("the resurrection is
past already") to Christian gnosticism—a trajectory
branded as heretical by the very church which had already
canonized John. Furthermore, the author of John clearly
had no conception of closed revelation but rather advocates
the on-going operation of the Spirit's witness.[19] The inclusion

[14]"Thoughts on the Present Controversy about Scriptural Interpretation," in
NTQT, 274-75.
[15]"The Canon of the New Testament and the Unity of the Church," in *ENTT*,
95 ff.
[16]"New Testament Questions of Today," in *NTQT*, 18.
[17]"Thoughts on the Present Controversy about Scriptural Interpretation," in
NTQT, 275.
[18]"The Canon of the New Testament and the Unity of the Church," in *ENTT*,
103-04.
[19]*The Testament of Jesus*, 75-76.

of this work in the canon suggests that those who framed the canon were not thoroughly consistent and rigidly logical in doing their work and that we in our own time ought not to take the canon as some kind of religious ultimate. Over against those who would identify canon and gospel, Käsemann maintains that the Bible is holy only when, and to the extent that, the Lord speaks out of it.[20] Käsemann invites us to test the spirits even within Scripture itself: "We are placed in a situation *vis-à-vis* Scripture which is both responsibility and freedom, for the Word has no existence in the realm of the objective, that is, outside our act of decision."[21] This clearly is the principle of the "canon within the canon" for which Käsemann has been so vigorously attacked. Yet when all is said and done, we may ask what theologian has not weighted parts of Scripture over other parts. Käsemann at least has the forthrightness and honesty to tell us that he thinks Paul is the most perceptive and accurate interpreter of what lies at the heart of Christianity.

Churches of the New Testament

Having discussed Käsemann's more general ideas concerning NT ecclesiology and the canon of Scripture, we are now in a better position to appreciate how he sees the different NT ecclesiastical structures and self-understandings found in Jewish Christianity, Hellenistic enthusiasm, Paul, "early catholicism," Hebrews, and John. But before we can even talk of Jewish Christianity we must recount Käsemann's views on the historical Jesus question.

As a student of Bultmann, Käsemann recognizes that Jesus meets us in the New Testament not as he was in himself but as the Lord of the community which believes in

---

[20]"Thoughts on the Present Controversy about Scriptural Interpretation," in *NTQT*, 273.
[21]"Is the Gospel Objective?" in *ENTT*, 58.

him.[22] He realizes that primitive Christianity was not primarily interested in the brute facts of the past as such, but was engaged in eliciting from the past the essence both of its faith and its own history.[23] Yet in spite of all this Käsemann thinks it remarkable that the community tenaciously maintained the identity of the exalted Lord with the earthly Jesus.[24] Furthermore, Käsemann maintains that we really can know something of the historical Jesus by applying the canon of dissimilarity: A statement can be ascribed to Jesus "when there are no grounds either for deriving tradition from Judaism or for ascribing it to primitive Christianity."[25] In the light of the first, second, and fourth antitheses of Mt 5, Jesus appears as one who rivals and challenges the authority of Moses and so has *ipso facto* set himself above Moses.[26] Jesus' attitude toward the Law is dialectical in that, while pursuing the will of God, he shatters the letter of that Law.[27] Furthermore, from an analysis of the *basileia* sayings Käsemann notes that Jesus does not refer primarily to an end of the world which can be dated chronologically. The Baptist's message concerning the remote God who is to come as judge recedes into the background, and apocalyptic dreams of a final holy war now seem absurd. For Jesus there can be no separation between the God who is near and the God who is far off—between the judge and the creator. Rather Jesus calls man to serve God in his daily life and to love his brother. Because he viewed all life as "before God" he did not baptize or build up a "holy remnant" or add to the Law.[28]

However, in the light of Easter the early Jewish-Christian church applied to Jesus the title "Son of Man." In fact, the return of Jesus as the heavenly Son of Man became the central hope which the disciples derived directly from the

---

[22]"The Problem of the Historical Jesus," in *ENTT*, 23.
[23]*ENTT*, 33.
[24]*ENTT*, 46.
[25]*ENTT*, 37.
[26]*ENTT*, 37.
[27]*ENTT*, 38.
[28]"On the Subject of Primitive Christian Apocalyptic," in *NTQT*, 112-14.

Easter experience and constituted their own peculiar Easter faith. The Easter-events were understood as the dawn of the general resurrection and were interpreted in the categories of apocalyptic.[29] The Christian community now regarded itself as the holy remnant mediating the covenant with the people of the twelve tribes. The healings and ecstasies occurring within this community are seen as the signs preceding the eschaton. The churches are governed by apostles (who are the pillars of the heavenly city of God) and by prophets.[30] Against E. Fuchs,[31] Käsemann argues that the problem of the Law did not emerge from reflection on Jesus' own preaching but from the unexpected success of the Gentile mission. This fact challenged the usual apocalyptic notion that when the people of God would be restored in the messianic age, only then would the nations be gathered to the twelve tribes in the New Jerusalem.[32]

Thus, according to Käsemann, the beginnings of Christian theology are to be traced to the disciples' response to Easter. The only response possible for them was in terms of apocalyptic language and categories.[33] While faith before Easter was essentially personal response in hearing the Word and in discipleship, after Easter faith becomes the appropriation of "acts of salvation" such as the cross, the resurrection, forgiveness and the new covenant, and presupposes a developed eschatology, Christology and ecclesiology.[34] Käsemann adds that apocalyptic may well have been the appropriate response to the fact that in Jesus the ultimate promise of the world is encountered. For the disciples the ultimate in authority was necessarily the ultimate in time, the destroyer of death and the inaugurator of the new age.[35]

[29]*NTQT,* 114-15.
[30]*NTQT,* 116.
[31]E. Fuchs, "On the Task of a Christian Theology," *Journal for Theology and the Church* 6 (1969) 69-98.
[32]"On the Subject of Primitive Christian Apocalyptic," in *NTQT,* 117-19.
[33]*NTQT,* 124.
[34]*NTQT,* 120.
[35]*NTQT,* 124.

As Christianity spread to more Hellenized lands, the categories of Jewish-Christian apocalyptic underwent a large-scale transformation. In the church at Corinth we find an eschatological enthusiasm which prescinds not only from the expectation of an imminent end but also from any theologically relevant future hope. This enthusiasm was basically a sacramental realism which saw complete redemption to have been effected already in that by baptism a heavenly spiritual body has been conferred and the earthly body has been degraded to an insubstantial, transitory veil.[36] Jesus is now seen as *Kyrios Christos*—the Lord of the world who already rules over the principalities and powers.

In coming to grips with the enthusiasts of Corinth Paul refuses to set aside future eschatology. Rather he maintains that participation in the resurrection remains in the future; while baptism may equip one for it and calls one to it, baptism does not itself convey the gift.[37] Though the resurrection of Christ constitutes the beginning of the general resurrection, it is still the great exception in which we can as yet participate by hope alone.[38] Behind this view is the fact that even after he became a Christian Paul remained an apocalyptist but shifted his perspectives from Israel's future hopes to the world as a whole. For Paul the *dikaiosynē theou* is God's sovereignty over the world revealing itself eschatologically in Jesus. The "faithful" are the world as it has been recalled to the sovereignty of God, the company of those who live under the eschatological justice of God, in which company the righteousness of God becomes manifest on earth.[39]

In view of this orientation and as a creative response to the threat of enthusiasm, Paul builds up charismatic communities. The Pauline churches are composed of members who are all, within their possibilities, at the same time priests and officeholders—instruments of the Spirit for the

[36]*NTQT,* 125-26.
[37]*NTQT,* 132.
[38]*NTQT,* 134.
[39]" 'The Righteousness of God' in Paul," in *NTQT,* 180-81; see the response of R. Bultmann, "*Diakaiosynē Theou,*" *JBL* 83 (1964) 12-16.

enactment of the gospel in the everyday world.[40] Charisms form the basis of all ministry, for charisms are the individuation of grace, the personal participation in the *pneuma* and the concretion of the Christian calling.[41] Indeed all charisms exist because they are all related to the charism of God which is eternal life in Christ Jesus.[42] Charisms are the common endowment of all who call upon the name of the Lord[43] and liberate the Christian for new obedience within a specific range of possibilities.[44] Since charisms are only manifested as genuine in the act of ministry, so only he who ministers to others can have authority and that only in the actual exercise of ministry.[45]

We might ask how Paul perceives his own charism. In explaining 1 Cor 9:14-18, where Paul refuses to accept rewards for his ministry because he has undertaken this under a compulsion (*anankē*), Käsemann suggests that Paul's attitude can be described as a Christian version of the Stoic *amor fati*. The divine will radically and successfully challenges man and makes its servant an instrument.[46] Yet this compulsion does not exclude love; rather it is "the power of the gospel liberating man for the service of his neighbor and moving him to love because he had been loved."[47] In another passage (2 Cor 10 — 13) Paul refuses to accept the criteria of his opponents—strength, miracles, eyewitness to the historical Jesus, approval by the church of Jerusalem, and so on. Because Paul understands his apostolate as a gift of grace, he needs no human legitimation.[48] His total obedience to the Lord and his total freedom are expressed in his charism which issues in service.[49]

---

[40]"Paul and Early Catholicism," in *NTQT*, 246.
[41]"Ministry and Community in the New Testament," *ENTT*, 80.
[42]*ENTT*, 64.
[43]*ENTT*, 73.
[44]*ENTT*, 78.
[45]*ENTT*, 78.
[46]"A Pauline Version of the 'Amor Fati'," in *NTQT*, 230.
[47]*NTQT*, 234.
[48]*Die Legitimatät des Apostels. Eine Untersuchung zu II Korinther 10—13* (Darmstadt: Wissenschaftliche Buchgesellschaft, 1956) 58.
[49]*Ibid.*, 61.

Worship in the Pauline communities depends neither on institutional persons with special prerogatives nor on fixed rites which would assure validity, but rather on the gathered community orientated towards word and sacrament as the sole and sufficient external guarantee.[50] Yet worship for Paul is not confined to, nor even primarily concerned with, rites. Taking over the Hellenistic notion that a man endowed with *pneuma* is able to offer spiritual worship,[51] Paul maintains that the Spirit imposes himself on the everyday life of the world as being the *locus* of our service of God.[52] Indeed the offering of our bodies as spiritual worship mentioned in Rom 12:1-2 describes what it means to stand under the righteousness of God.[53]

The notions of charism, ministry and worship which we have discussed are all ultimately founded in Paul's doctrine of the body of Christ. The body of Christ is not a mere metaphor or image, nor can it be explained through the OT notion of corporate personality or the Stoic concept of the "All." The idea (which is not original to Paul) is based on the myth of the archetypal man, who is also the redeemer, with his immense body.[54] Whatever the origins of this concept, the body of Christ proved attractive to Paul because it expressed better than the notion of the "people of God" the motif of a new creation with a world-wide dimension.[55] Incorporation into the body is not the quantitative sum of all the members, but the qualitative identity of Christ with himself in all his members.[56] This means that a single congregation can be addressed as the body of Christ.[57] Furthermore, it implies that Paul is not interested in the church as a religious

---

[50] "Ministry and Community in the New Testament," 80.
[51] "Worship in Everyday Life," in *NTQT,* 190.
[52] "Principles of the Interpretation of Romans 13," in *NTQT,* 212.
[53] "Worship in Everyday Life," 189.
[54] "The Pauline Doctrine of the Lord's Supper," in *ENTT,* 130.
[55] "Das theologische Problem des Motivs vom Leibe Christi," in *Paulinische Perspektiven* (Tübingen: Mohr-Siebeck, 1969) 189.
[56] "The Pauline Doctrine of the Lord's Supper," 111.
[57] *ENTT,* 111.

organization but is concerned with it only in so far as the church is the "means through" which Christ reveals himself on earth and is embodied through his Spirit in the world.[58]

Through baptism and the Eucharist the Lord comes to us, takes possession of us and claims us for his own.[59] The spirit or *pneuma,* which in Hellenistic thought is heavenly matter penetrating man's being and endowing him with a new nature,[60] is imparted in these sacraments; thus the exalted Lord conveys, along with his gift, participation in himself as the Giver.[61] The bodily self-imparting of Christ in the sacraments (especially the Eucharist) claims us for concrete obedience in our bodies within the body of Christ.[62]

The Pauline understanding of office, worship, Christian freedom, and responsibility was unable to control the ferment of enthusiasm in the churches. It seems rather to have made the situation more critical. Out of a pressing need for which it knew no other remedy, the church grasped at those forms of church government which had stood the test in Jewish Christianity.[63] So there emerged a form of Christianity which Käsemann describes as "early catholicism." By early catholicism he refers to the so-called ancient church as seen in Luke-Acts, the Pastoral Epistles, Ephesians, Jude, and 2 Peter.[64] The phenomenon is marked by the disappearance of the expectation of an imminent end and by the appearance of the message about the world-pervading church as the reality of the kingdom of Christ on earth. For Paul the church is the creation of the Word, while for "early catholicism" the church is the possessor of truth and the mother of the faithful. Paul relies on the priesthood of all believers and worships in the secularity of the world, but "early catholicism" demands a sacramentally guaranteed

---

[58]"Das theologische Problem . . . ," 204.
[59]"The Pauline Doctrine . . . ," 118.
[60]*ENTT,* 115.
[61]*ENTT,* 114.
[62]*ENTT,* 135.
[63]"Paul and Early Catholicism," in *NTQT,* 247.
[64]*NTQT,* 237.

office and develops its own cult. Paul maintains the hope of eschatological intervention while "early catholicism" takes refuge in salvation-history and the spread of Christianity. Freedom and the mission guide Paul's ethic; uniformity and self-admiration underlay the moral teaching of "early catholicism."[65]

"Early catholicism" for Käsemann presupposes a church that has expanded across the world as well as a church which is consolidating itself internally, a church which separates itself from its environment sociologically and ideologically.[66] The church itself becomes the content of theology.[67] This kind of thinking rests on the convictions that the plan of salvation is to be discerned in history and that continuity with the holy origins legitimates the church. The training of the congregation is entrusted to a fixed circle, and pastors exercise the administrative functions which will soon fall to the bishops.[68] The Spirit is restricted to the *Una sancta,* and the bestowal of the Spirit to the laying-on of hands.[69] The authority of the institutional ministry stands guaranteed by a principle of tradition and legitimate succession; Luke even goes so far as to identify the apostles with the companions of Jesus. The ministry itself becomes surrounded with various executive organs in the shape of the presbyterate, the diaconate and the order of widows.[70] 2 Peter, composed presumably in the middle of the second century, reflects the theological outcome of these various "early catholic" structures. Faith becomes the saved state of the citizens of heaven; while this state belongs primarily to the apostles of Jesus as the specially elect, it overflows from them to other believers.[71] Revelation is now

[65] *NTQT,* 250.
[66] "Ephesians and Acts," in *Studies in Luke-Acts. Essays presented in honor of Paul Schubert,* (Nashville/New York: Abingdon, 1966) 290.
[67] *Ibid.,* 290.
[68] *Ibid.,* 292-93.
[69] "The Disciples of John the Baptist in Ephesus," in *ENTT,* 143.
[70] "Ministry and Community in the New Testament," in *ENTT,* 88-90.
[71] "An Apologia for Primitive Christian Eschatology," in *ENTT,* 174.

a deposit or a piece of property at the church's disposal.[72] The apostle becomes the guarantor of the tradition, the witness to the sacred history, the pillar of an institution which dispenses salvation, the man who brings security.[73] Eschatology is reduced to a doctrine of retribution by which the future judge of the world rewards and punishes.[74]

What assessment of "early catholicism" does Käsemann present? In the historical situation "early catholicism" was probably an adequate response under the Spirit to the threat of enthusiasm. By binding the Spirit to church office and by emphasizing the fiction of continuity the church survived and attained some measure of stability in a troubled time. [75] Still, according to Käsemann, this structure and the theology which undergirds it ought not to be absolutized. A church which proves so concerned to defend itself against heretics that it cannot distinguish between Spirit and letter, that it identifies the gospel with its own tradition and a particular world-view, that regulates exegesis according to its system of teaching authority, that makes faith into a mere assent to the dogmas of orthodoxy, can hardly be the church of Jesus Christ.[76] Furthermore, Paul's concept of church which Käsemann finds so attractive cannot possibly be harmonized with that which comes to prevail in "early catholicism"; he feels that "early catholicism" is in starkest contradiction to it.[77]

Two other communities represented by Hebrews and John respectively exist on the periphery of the developing "great church." Using Heb 3:7 — 4:13 as a starting point, Käsemann shows how the community understands itself as the people of God forced to wander in the wilderness like Israel of old and to overcome trials in an effort to remain

[72]*ENTT*, 174.
[73]*ENTT*, 177.
[74]*ENTT*, 181.
[75]"Paul and Early Catholicism," 247.
[76]"An Apologia . . . ," 195.
[77]"Ministry and Community . . . ," 92.

faithful to the promise. The key word in Hebrews is *epangelia,* which the author seems to use as the equivalent of "gospel" and "covenant." While the community now shares in the promise, the goal of its wandering is the fulfillment of the eschatological promise which is described as *katapausis* ("repose" or "rest").[78] The OT people of God did not achieve the goal because it sought God through the cult here on earth, whereas he could only be encountered in the heavenly cult of which Jesus is the high priest.[79]

Behind this concept of the community is the motif (also found in Philo and gnosticism) of a way on which the people of God wander and which leads through the world to heaven.[80] The Christology of Hebrews is similar to that of the early Christian hymns preserved in Phil 2:5-11, Col 1:15-20, and 1 Tim 3:16.[81] Christ as the first-born Son of God guarantees that the wandering people of God will be saved and will reach its goal so long as it does not fall away.[82] He is their leader (*archēgos*), and cultic confession of Jesus summons the people of God to follow Christ on the way.[83] It is in this manner that the community of Hebrews experienced Jesus, and so it was led to depict him as its perfecter and leader on the path to final rest.

Composed in the late first century possibly in Syria, John (according to Käsemann) represents an idiosyncratic and aberrant theology in direct opposition to everything resembling the Lukan "time of the church." The author is not concerned with past happenings in history, salvation-history or even future eschatology, but with the presence of Christ now.[84] For John the church is basically and exclusively the fellowship of people who hear Jesus' word and

---

[78] *Das wandernde Gottesvolk. Eine Untersuchung zum Hebräerbrief* (Göttingen: Vändenhoeck & Ruprecht, 1939) 27.

[79] *Ibid.,* 37.

[80] *Ibid.,* 51.

[81] *Ibid.,* 70.

[82] *Ibid.,* 73.

[83] *Ibid.,* 110.

[84] "The Structure and Purpose of the Prologue to John's Gospel," in *ENTT,* 165.

believe in him; it is the community under the Word.[85] By playing down Peter and the other major disciples and by introducing new figures such as Nathaniel, Nicodemus, Lazarus, and Thomas, and women like the Samaritan woman, Mary and Martha, and Mary Magdalene, John cleverly eliminates the theological significance of the apostles as a unique group.[86] Furthermore, the community is viewed from the aspect of its individual members rather than from its corporate dimension.[87] Also, the author does not seem to regard the church as an institution of salvation.[88] The witness of the Old Testament, the word and work of the earthly Jesus and the church's dogmatic proclamations are all merely historical aspects of the revelation of the Logos who is one with the Father.[89] John identifies the Spirit with the voice of Jesus which in the form of the Paraclete continues to speak from heaven to the disciples when he himself is no longer with them.[90]

For John brotherly love means seeing one's brother as existing under the Word of God, receiving him through the Word and giving him the possibility of remaining under the Word. Brotherly love is heavenly solidarity directed toward individual Christians.[91] Unity on earth exists as a reflection and extension of heavenly reality, and so the community itself is a heavenly reality.[92] In this perspective the Christian mission means seeking out brothers through the proclamation of the Word which proceeds from God to Christ and thence to the community.[93] Finally, John sees the community as exposed to satanic attacks from the outside and as capable of resistance only through the power of Christ.[94]

[85] *The Testament of Jesus. A Study of the Gospel of John in the Light of Chapter 17* (Philadelphia: Fortress, 1968) 40.
[86] *Ibid.,* 29.
[87] *Ibid.,* 31.
[88] *Ibid.,* 44.
[89] *Ibid.,* 43.
[90] *Ibid.,* 46.
[91] *Ibid.,* 70.
[92] *Ibid.,* 69.
[93] *Ibid.,* 70.
[94] *Ibid.,* 52.

While we would naturally like to know more about certain aspects of the churches which produced Hebrews and John (for example, Did they have sacraments? Was there a formalized ministry?), we must be satisfied with what we can learn from the sources. Indeed it would also be valuable to have as much information about Jewish Christianity and Hellenistic enthusiasm as we do about the Pauline churches and "early catholicism."

At any rate, we should be thankful to Käsemann for his many extraordinarily rich insights into matters such as the diversity of ecclesial structures in the New Testament, the importance of freedom in the church, the theological problem of the canon, Jesus' preaching, eschatological language as a response to Easter, Paul's understanding of apocalyptic and charism, "early catholicism" as an entity, the church as the wandering people of God and as the community under the Word. All of these are essential aspects of NT thought, but probably no one has brought them out as clearly and dramatically as Käsemann has.

Critical Reflections

In the first part of this article we were concerned with Ernst Käsemann's positive contributions to our understanding of the church in the New Testament. We singled out as of special interest his descriptions of the various church structures and his emphasis on diversity in the early church. Now, at the risk of appearing ungrateful, we must question certain of Käsemann's theological views in an effort to understand him better and in the hope of grasping contemporary Catholic positions and directions in greater depth and clarity. There are several matters of historical detail which could be explored. What is the logical validity of reconstructing the teaching of Jesus on the basis of the canon of dissimilarity alone? While application of this canon tells us much about what distinguished Jesus from his contemporaries, it remains unsatisfactory. Could this criterion ever yield a consensus as to what sayings must necessarily come from Jesus?[95] Does not this criterion gratuitously assume a discontinuity between Jesus and the church?[96] Logically, the principle of dissimilarity gives greater probability to certain sayings as having no other probable source but Jesus, yet Jesus could also have repeated many things he considered true from his culture. Furthermore, what is the relation between Jesus and the church? According to Käsemann, Jesus emphasized the "present" aspect of inaugurated eschatology while the Palestinian church seized upon its future dimensions. If this is so, can Jesus be said to have founded the church?[97] Käsemann does not explicitly say that Jesus did not found the church, but he does suggest that some aspects of the earliest church were misinterpretations of Jesus's message. Also, enthusiasm remains always a dark figure lurking in the background but is never really explained in detail. In fact, Käsemann may be seeing polemic in New Testament passages where there is none at all. At any rate, enthusiasm does appear to be too much of a catch-all to inspire the historian's confidence. For example, one can readily suggest further reasons for the emergence of "early catholicism" than the reaction against enthusiasm— the passing of the pioneers, the growth of the church, persecution from outside the church. While conflict is often the

---

[95]On K's contribution to the New Quest for the historical Jesus, see R. Batey, "Ernst Käsemann's Question Concerning the Historical Jesus," *Restoration Quarterly* 10 (1967) 196-200 and R.S. Barbour, "Theologians of our Time XX. Ernst Käsemann and Gunther Bornkamm," *ExpT* 76 (1965) 379-83. See also J. M. Robinson, *A New Quest of the Historical Jesus* (SBT 25; London: SCM, 1959); P. J. Cahill, "Rudolf Bultmann and Post-Bultmann Tendencies," *CBQ* 24 (1964) 153-78; H. Zahrnt, *The Question of God. Protestant Theology in the Twentieth Century*, (New York: Harcourt, Brace & World, 1969) 253-94.

[96]F. G. Downing, *The Church and Jesus. A Study in History, Philosophy and Theology* (SBT 2/10; London: SCM, 1968) 116.

[97]See H. Küng, *The Church* (New York: Sheed and Ward, 1967) 70-79. See also J. Reumann, *Jesus in the Church's Gospels: Modern Scholarship and the Earliest Sources* (Philadelphia: Fortress, 1968) 306-14.

motor of change, perhaps Käsemann overemphasized the church's struggle against enthusiasm. Finally and most seriously, Käsemann does seem to overestimate the transfer value of New Testament theology to the modern situation. One cannot escape the impression that underlying much of Käsemann's work is the analogy: Paul is to "early catholicism" as the authentic Lutheran teaching on justification is to the institutional churches.

But we are more interested now in examining the broader theological issues implicit in Käsemann's life-long study of the New Testament church. The areas which we have chosen to follow up are these: (1) Why does Käsemann see "early catholicism" as a retrogression rather than a development? (2) Must we be satisfied to see the canon as the principle of diversity (and disunity) for the church today, or can we find a creative theological use for the "whole canon?" (3) To what extent is diversity considered an ideal in the New Testament churches? (4) What significance does Paul's notion of charismatic ministry hold for the church today?

Both the order and the nature of the questions asked in the preceding paragraph reveal my own purpose and orientation in this part of the article. Rather than choosing an historical or logical order, I have tried to arrive at a sequence which will best contribute to our understanding of Käsemann's theological stance. In making my own observations and criticisms I am not under the illusion that I am "correcting" or "refuting" Käsemann. Since Käsemann has spent most of his academic career depicting the diversity and pluriformity of belief and practice in the early church, he would hardly be overwhelmed by my differing positions. In fact, I raise these issues only because they highlight Käsemann's own achievement and challenge other theologians to express their views on some very important matters in ecclesiology.

"Early Catholicism" as Retrogression

When the non-German examines Käsemann's positions on the New Testament church, he can feel like an observer at a debate where the second party has failed to appear. He can be mystified by the vehemence and conviction with which Käsemann holds certain positions. Why does he see "early catholicism" as a retrogression rather than as a development? Why is he so insistent on distinguishing the gospel from the Jewish and Hellenistic elements of the New Testament world? Perhaps Käsemann himself gives us the answer to these questions when he describes his own theological education. In a recent essay Käsemann mentions how he studied dialectic theology, how he freed himself from the reigning historicist-idealism of the day, and how through this theology he came to recognize the real meaning of the Reformation teaching on justification by faith. The perspective of dialectic theology immunized him against the salvation-history concept which was to be secularized and politicized by the Third Reich. He is still suspicious of any renewal of this mode of theology.[98] Dialectic theology, which arose in part as a reaction to the catastrophe of World War I, proclaimed that God is totally different from fallen man, that faith rather than reason is man's only access to God, and that Jesus Christ in his crucifixion is the single sign of God's approach to man.

The other debater seems to be the ghost of Hegel. For Hegel history is the temporal march of absolute spirit through the world, and thus somehow everything in history constitutes a divine revelation. Even though some events may seem to contradict the divine purpose, the broad sweep

---

[98]"Rechtfertigung und Heilsgeschichte in Römerbrief," in *Paulinische Perspektiven,* 114-15.

of history amply justifies God's purposes. As *Logos* Jesus is the self-actualization and self-manifestation of the absolute mind. In Jesus the Infinite has been completely actualized in the finite. Jesus gave expression to that which is universal and which is potentially true of every being. The Incarnation allows Christianity to be worldly and visible.[99] The effect of this debate between Hegel's ghost (as seen in major figures of the historical school such as von Harnack and Jülicher) and dialectic theology can be glimpsed concretely by comparing the *Meyer Kommentar* volumes on 1 Cor published by J. Weiss in 1910 and by H. Conzelmann in 1969. Inspired by the theology of his day, Weiss emphasized the relations between the Christian and Greek spirit and between early Christian and Hellenistic piety. Writing from the background of the dialectic theologies of Barth and Bultmann, Conzelmann sees Paul as the theologian of the cross who struggles to prevent its being replaced by any human standard of culture.[100] One hesitates to group under one label such diverse figures as Käsemann, Conzelmann, Barth, and Bultmann, but it does seem helpful to recognize how they all are reacting against a common theological and philosophical heritage.

It is indeed intriguing to place many of Käsemann's most tenaciously held positions against this background of dialectic theology especially in its early developments.[101] This comparison is made only to locate Käsemann's positions and to assist us in understanding why he may hold the views which he does. (1) Käsemann's effort to extricate the gospel from human culture reminds one of F. Gogarten's statement that Christendom "as the external, original deed of God, of course, transcends history and continues to do so, and that everything depends on its not being mixed and confused

[99]See now J. C. O'Neill, "Bultmann and Hegel," *JTS* 21 (1970) 388-400.

[100]U. Wilckens, "Paulus-Kommentare zweier theologischer Epochen," *Evangelische Kommentar* 3 (1970) 246-47.

[101]A convenient collection in English is J. M. Robinson (ed.), *The Beginnings of Dialectic Theology I* (Richmond, VA: John Knox, 1968). For a popular history of the movement, see H. Zahrnt, *The Question of God*.

with its historical effects."[102] K. Barth argued that "the faith which is awakened by God will never be able fully to avoid the necessity of a more or less 'radical' protest against this world ... "[103] Finally, Bultmann observed that "the danger of all culture is that it idolizes and absolutizes one particular cultural position, and this empties man's self."[104] (2) Käsemann's view that history is not necessarily progress and development recalls Bultmann's statement:

> The moments of religious experience form no orderly correspondence either causally or teleologically. They do not develop cumulatively or in a single direction, so that one generation could solve a religious problem for the next, and new problems develop organically like the statements of mathematics or law or art ... Religious experiences do not stand in developmental relation to one another; either they are there or not, and they are always fundamentally the same.[105]

A. Jülicher, who along with von Harnack led the initial historicist opposition to dialectic theology, even accused Gogarten and Barth of saying that "there is no more progress in history, that development is forever at an end, and that no optimism in the interest of culture moves us anymore."[106] While this is an overstatement, Jülicher correctly recognized that the dialectic theologians had no illusions about the view of history as the temporal march of absolute spirit through the world. (3) Käsemann's insistence on diverse church groups, with unity as a purely eschatological property, recalls Bultmann's statement:

> The ideal is not, in fact, the institution of a well-organized church, which includes all citizens, a people's church, but

---

[102]F. Gogarten, "The Holy Egoism of the Christian. An Answer to Jülicher's Essay: A Modern Interpreter of Paul," in *Beginnings*, 83.

[103]K. Barth, "Fifteen Answers to Professor von Harnack," in *Beginnings*, 168.

[104]R. Bultmann, "Religion and Culture," in *Beginnings*, 219.

[105]*Ibid.*, 214.

[106]A. Jülicher, "A Modern Interpreter of Paul," in *Beginnings*, 79.

rather small, active communities, free churches, above which is the one, invisible, true church, to which all the truly pious belong.[107]

(4) Finally, Käsemann's insistence that the church must not be absolutized echoes Bultmann's remark made in his debate with Erik Peterson. Bultmann complained that by relating the Holy Spirit to the church Peterson had effectively excluded that Spirit: ". . . the seriousness of God remains reserved to God himself and can never be delegated once for all to an earthly entity, even if it be the church."[108] It is ironic that Käsemann has recently levelled the charge of making the church the object of faith against Bultmann himself.[109]

This series of quotations from the early writings of dialectic theology helps us to see more clearly Käsemann's own position in the history of theology and, more specifically, why he is not impressed by the claim that "early catholicism" is an important development under the guidance of the Spirit. While he will admit that "early catholicism" was an adequate response to a particular historical situation, he cannot endow this stage in the church's history with any absolute validity. Rather he wishes to return to the heart of Christian faith which he finds expressed in Paul's teaching of righteousness by faith alone. Käsemann's theological views were reinforced by his experiences during the Nazi period. As a pastor, his sermons were often delivered under Gestapo surveillance, and as a consequence of one sermon he even spent a brief time in prison. Thus there is little in either his theological education or his personal experience to inspire confidence in salvation-history or the church's identification with culture.

---

[107]Bultmann, "Religion and Culture," 213.

[108]Bultmann, "The Question of 'Dialectic' Theology: A Discussion with Erik Peterson," in *Beginnings,* 263.

[109]"Blind Alleys in the 'Jesus of History' Controversy," *NTQT,* 57-58.

The Theological Problem of the Canon

We noted previously that Käsemann does not consider all Scripture to be on the same level but urges us to discern the Spirit in the various writings and to determine how the Word speaks to us today. We also suggested that he finds Paul's teaching of righteousness by faith alone to be at the heart of the Christian message while he reckons other writings especially those of "early catholicism," to be retrogressions. For Käsemann and many other German Lutheran theologians the gospel has been obscured even in the New Testament through Hellenistic, Jewish, gnostic, and "early catholic" influences. Therefore, Scripture can be judged as gospel insofar as it conforms to the primitive kerygma (the gospel) and to the doctrine of justification by faith according to Paul and the Reformers.[110] Thus, the products of "early catholicism," far from being a progress or a development under the inspiration of the Spirit, are seen as a departure or a falling-away from the gospel and as such can hardly serve as the foundation for an authentic Christian theology.

Catholic reaction to Käsemann's "canon within the canon" has been somewhat predictable. N. Appel contrasted the Reformation's *sola scriptura* with the Catholic refusal to separate Scripture from the church which produced it and the Reformation's *solus Christus* with the Catholic view that the church is the extension (body) of Christ in the world.[111] He saw the roots of the "canon within the canon" in Luther's dictum: *Quod si adversarii scripturam urserint contra Christum, urgemus Christum contra scripturam.*[112] Furthermore, Appel emphasized that discern-

---

[110]N. Appel, *Kanon und Kirche. Die Kanonkrise im heutigen Protestantismus als kontroverstheologisches Problem* (Paderborn: Bonafacius, 1962) 333-37. Käsemann has recently assembled 15 major essays on the theological problem of the canon and added his own comments; see *Das Neue Testament als Kanon. Dokumentation und kritische Analyse zur gegenwärtigen Diskussion* (Göttingen: Vandenhoeck & Ruprecht, 1970).

[111]Appel, 352-56.

[112]Appel, 236.

ing the Spirit in the Scriptures is not purely an individual task but is the result of the church's corporate activity.[113] H. Küng maintained that a *Catholic* attitude preserves a full openness and freedom with respect to the whole New Testament.[114] Although the New Testament must be historically differentiated and translated in terms of the present, the whole New Testament must be given full value.[115] While Küng's attitude sounds attractive initially, it remains ultimately quite romantic and idealistic. Käsemann is correct in admitting that we all interpret the New Testament through some spectacles (whether they are those of "early catholicism," Protestant justification by faith alone, or whatever), and so it seems foolish to deny that the "canon within the canon" is a working principle for all theologians. Even Küng himself in his book *The Church* distinguishes between primary Christian sources and secondary Christian sources (such as the epistle of James).[116]

The further problem for theologians is to discover what creative theological use can be discovered in the church's "whole" canon. Must the canon be a dead weight for the church? Must it be something to be explained away? Must it continue to be a source of disunity? Perhaps we can begin to answer these questions by reflecting on the way in which the canon itself was formed.[117] In establishing the canon the church authorities of the second and succeeding centuries ratified the use (especially liturgical) of certain books by the Christian communities. The organized church as such did not create the canon; it only recognized the canon which had

---

[113]Appel, 358-60.

[114]H. Küng, *Structures of the Church* (New York: Nelson, 1964) 164; see also "Der Frühkatholizismus im Neuen Testament als kontroverstheologisches Problem," *Theologische Quartalschrift* 142 (1962) 385-424.

[115]Küng, *Structures,* 168.

[116]H. Küng, *The Church* (London: Burns and Oates, 1967) 294. This excellent book reveals how much Küng (and through him Catholic theologians) have learned from K. While Küng's early debates with K were highly polemical, he has now managed to integrate many of K's insights into his own thinking.

[117]For historical surveys of this process see Appel, 17-265 and H. von Campenhausen, *Die Entstehung der christlichen Bibel* (Tübingen: Mohr-Siebeck, 1968).

been created.[118] The real norm for accepting books was the extent to which the writing expressed the sound faith of the community and proved its power as such. Only later did anything like imposition "from above" (i.e. from the hierarchy) arise.

Clearly then, the books of the canon are "church books." Therefore, the issue underlying the whole discussion about the canon is this: Is the New Testament an historically fortuitous collection of early Christian writings or can we detect a theological meaning in the given boundaries of the canon?[119] Suppose we choose the latter option. According to this view the Spirit was acting not only by aiding the church to develop the structures of "early catholicism" as a response to a particular historical crisis but also by inspiring it to accept the writings of "early catholicism" as being of permanent value. A church which sees the limits of the canon as theologically significant should feel challenged by the discordant voices in that canon and impelled to explore the meaning of those voices. In a way this church stands under the canon of Scripture and so must constantly reassess its own usage in the light of those biblical theologies which it has not followed in order to be certain that what God meant to teach through such theological views will not be lost.[120] For example, if the church decides not to translate the charismatic theology of Paul into an ecclesial structure, it must first be able to say what is useful and what is inadequate in Pauline ecclesiology.

This observation suggests that there is a danger in muting too quickly certain voices which the church has long found normative. By elevating the "canon within the canon" to the

---

[118]K. Aland, *The Problem of the New Testament Canon* (London: Mowbray, 1962) 18.

[119]G. C. Chapman, "Ernst Käsemann, Hermann Diem, and the New Testament Canon," *JAAR* 36 (1968) 11.

[120]R. E. Brown, "Canonicity" in *Jerome Biblical Commentary* II (Englewood Cliffs: Prentice Hall, 1968) 533. A good example of this process can be seen in Y. Congar's review of Küng's *The Church* in *Revue des Sciences Philosophiques et Théologiques* 53 (1969) 693-706.

level of a theological principle we run the risk of intruding personal prejudgments and of precluding the possibility that a given biblical text may well be able to speak to church conditions and audiences different from our own.[121] The rediscovery of apocalyptic in the New Testament in which Käsemann himself has played such a significant role is a case in point. For years this material had been ignored and, more recently, demythologized; it was a source of embarrassment rather than enlightenment for Christian theologians. Now in our own age the "theology of hope" movement has taken New Testament apocalyptic seriously and worked out a stance which speaks very eloquently to modern Christians. Had theologians over the ages been willing to excise this apocalyptic material as a mere remnant of Jewish thought and therefore sub-Christian, we might have been incapable of formulating a sound theology for our own day.[122]

Unity and Diversity in the Church

Käsemann's position that the unity of the church remains primarily an eschatological property probably should be seen in connection with his views on the canon. Within the canon there are clearly different theologies and ecclesiologies; so diverse are these that it is hard to imagine John, Paul, and the author of Hebrews really understanding one another in any kind of detailed discussion. While Käsemann's work through the years has done much to demonstrate the lack of uniformity in New Testament thought, he may have underestimated the importance of unity in the New Testament church. Perhaps his attitude stems from a

---

[121]Chapman, 11-12.

[122]Even Ernst Bloch, the philosopher of this movement, derived his inspiration not only from Karl Marx but also from NT apocalyptic; see his essay "Incipit Vita Nova" in *Man on His Own* (New York: Herder and Herder, 1970) 73-92. See especially J. Moltmann, *Religion, Revolution and the Future* (New York: Harper & Row, 1969) 10.

realistic appraisal of a divided Christianity in Germany so that he has been led to absorb the theological notion of an invisible church. Whatever the genesis of this view, it does seem to contradict what we can learn from the New Testament itself.

There appear to be common elements of doctrine found in all the New Testament churches. From the very beginning the Christian communities were conscious of a continuity with Israel as well as a newness in Christ. Baptism and the Eucharist are found at all levels of New Testament thought; even if John "spiritualizes" these rites, he is certainly aware of them.[123] On the practical level, the willingness of the local churches to support others as evidenced by concern for widows and the poor and by the collection for the Jerusalem church indicates a spirit of unity. Furthermore, the specific ground for New Testament parenesis is often an appeal to unity. It is the one God who has called all, the one Lord to whom we all belong, the one Spirit who fills all and unites all, etc. The dominant images of the different New Testament ecclesiologies—the body in Paul, union in John, the people of God in Hebrews, the communion of saints in the Apocalypse—all rest on the conviction that the church has been formed into one by confession of faith in Jesus Christ and the Spirit.[124]

The argument we are trying to make against Käsemann now is that he seems to over-value diversity to the point that he makes of it an ideal. In fact, diversity is not a New Testament ideal. The existence of different churches in the New Testament provides no excuse for lack of unity among churches today. Of course, the unity about which we are speaking cannot be the subjection of one church to another; rather it means mutual acceptance and mutual respect.

[123]R. E. Brown, "The Unity and Diversity in New Testament Ecclesiology," *NovT* 6 (1963) 298-308.

[124]R. Schnackenburg, *The Church in the New Testament* (New York: Herder and Herder, 1965) 128-32. See also P.S. Minear, *Images of the Church in the New Testament* (Philadelphia: Westminster, 1960).

Unity is endangered only by hostile confrontation: "It is not the differences in themselves which are harmful, but only excluding and exclusive differences. Then these differences are endowed with unqualified validity and make Christian fellowship impossible."[125]

At this point it may be helpful to return to the matter of the canon. What are the theological implications of the "whole canon" for church unity today? We must first recall that the church which ratified the canon was ecumenical enough to embrace those who held very different theological views.[126] Perhaps this canon could still be a model or a pattern for ecumenical union.[127] Just as Käsemann can see the roots of Roman Catholicism in Luke-Acts and the other writings of "early catholicism," so other theologians have seen the biblical bases for Protestantism and Orthodoxy in Paul and John respectively. Would it not be truly creative for the various churches to recognize the canon as a concrete and hallowed way to mutual respect and as a practical path to the unification of Christian confessions? Perhaps these groups could begin from the formal canon and discern the principles by which they have arrived at their own "working" canons. Käsemann has carried this step of the process through with more consistency and honesty than most theologians have, but the further issue is: Should we be satisfied to remain within our "canons within the canon?" In fact, the "whole canon" principle ought to inspire us with understanding and tolerance for the canons of others.[128] This does not mean that we must finally adopt either Paul or

---

[125]Küng, *The Church,* 276.

[126]Brown, 533. This church showed less willingness to tolerate diversity on practical matters.

[127]E. Haible, "Der Kanon des Neuen Testaments als Modelfall einer kirchlichen Wiedervereinigung," *Trier Theologische Zeitschrift* 15 (1966) 11-27; M. Bouttier, "Catholicité et canonicité. Remarques sur un récent débat oecuménique," *Etudes Théologiques et Religieuses* 40 (1965) 181-92.

[128]Aland, 33. The point here as before, is this: While we may not escape the "canon within the canon" as a working principle, we should not necessarily make it a theological principle. Historically, even where the whole canon was accepted more or less in principle, certain NT books became more important for certain communities (for example, Mt over Paul in North Africa in the patristic period, etc.).

"early catholicism" as normative. It does mean that from open dialogue on the basis of both Paul and "early catholicism" we might come to a *tertium quid* which will be the authentic church of Christ for our age. Far from being the principle of church disunity, the canon may well be the means toward unity. Perhaps this kind of theological dialogue is what it really means to discern the Spirit in the Scriptures today; this process may also enable us to view the history of the Church with greater clarity and honesty.

Charism and Today's Church

That all this talk of theological dialogue on the basis of the canon need not be sheer speculation is verified by recent developments in the theology of ministry. While there are certainly other theological and sociological factors involved, the recent attempts at evolving a viable theology of ministry made by H. Küng[129] and G. Hasenhüttl[130] show how seriously German Catholic theologians have taken Käsemann's descriptions of ministry in the New Testament. This development also suggests that Käsemann may have over-emphasized the differences not only between Paul and "early catholicism" but also among Christian confessions today. One of Käsemann's best contributions to understanding the church in the New Testament has been the description of charism as the basis for ministry in the Pauline churches. Yet Käsemann notes wistfully that not even Protestantism has ever made a serious attempt to create a church order which reflected the Pauline doctrine of charisms, but has left this to the sects. "Early catholicism" recognized the weakness of this kind of church structure—it inevitably opens the doors to fanaticism.[131] Perhaps Käse-

---

[129]Küng, *The Church*, 363-480.

[130]G. Hasenhüttl, *Charisma. Ordnungsprinzip der Kirche* (Ökumenische Forschungen 5; Freiburg: Herder, 1969). See also K. Rahner, *The Dynamic Element in the Church* (Quaestiones Disputatae 12; New York: Herder, 1964).

[131]"Ministry and Community in the New Testament," in *ENTT*, 93.

mann has given up too easily here. The vast outpouring of books and articles on Christian ministry suggests that the traditional theological justifications are in trouble.[132] While we admit that modern sociologists might be horrified at the very thought of Paul's charismatic communities, and while we hesitate to propose a comprehensive theology for offices which have undergone so many radical changes through the years,[133] it does seem that Paul's notion of charism can provide the most adequate and profound basis for Christian ministry today.

As we mentioned before, possibly Käsemann has overemphasized the opposition between Paul and "early catholicism" and therefore also between charismatic and institutional communities. In the developing "charismatic" notion of ministry the following concepts can be listed as basic principles: (1) There is a dramatic need for leaders who incarnate the goals, values, and spirit of the church in all its facets. Equations between hierarchy and church, "career" and ministry, administration and leadership are all being rejected. (2) The diversity of church structures in the New Testament and differing lists of charisms there have led theologians to discern the content and form of charisms today rather than to try to reconstitute a New Testament church. This insight is a major step toward establishing a church whose marks are freedom and openness. (3) The terms "institutional" and "organizational" are being reinterpreted to mean (as they did for Paul) "contributing to the growth and orderly function of the church." This suggests that charism must find fulfillment in service: "Where there is a real charism, there will be responsible service for the edification and benefit of the community."[134] It also implies that authority in the church demands a genuine commitment to serve the members of the church and all mankind.

---

[132]See K. McDonnell, "Ways of Validating Ministry," *JES* 7 (1970) 209-65 and E. Schillebeeckx, "The Catholic Understanding of Office in the Church," *TS* 30 (1969) 567-87.

[133]See *The Ministry in Historical Perspectives,* ed. H. R. Niebuhr and D. D. Williams (New York: Harper, 1956).

[134]Küng, *The Church,* 394.

Conclusion

These reflections on the theological issues raised by Käsemann's understanding of the church in the New Testament have been offered to illumine the historical and theological background of his reconstructions. His theological education in dialectic theology and his experiences in the Nazi years raised the questions of the meaning of history and the relation between church and culture. The typically Lutheran search for the "gospel" within the New Testament and the reliance on the Pauline doctrine of righteousness by faith alone indicate Käsemann's confessional background. His experiences of the divisions within German Christianity may have led him to underestimate the importance of unity in the church. Finally, we noted the irony that Käsemann's work on charism may have already served to promote church unity in the area of ministry.

Yet these observations are not meant solely to draw attention to the theological achievement of a distinguished scholar. They also serve to sharpen some important questions facing contemporary theologians. How can we describe the history of the church as development or progress? Must the canon be ignored or can we find creative theological uses for it? How can we go about the task of promoting church unity in the future? How can we find theological justifications for Christian ministry in the modern world? At the beginning of the article we noted how often Käsemann has determined the questions and initiated debate in various areas of research (for example, the new quest for the historical Jesus, apocalypticism, the canon, unity and the diversity in the New Testament churches, and "early catholicism"). We trust that he will continue to do so for years to come. We also hope that English-speaking theologians of the future will take his life's work on the church into account and grapple with the issues raised by this remarkable scholar.

2. BAPTISM IN THE HOLY SPIRIT

Perhaps the brightest sign of life in the American Catholic Church today is the rise of groups which gather together for prayer and describe themselves as "Pentecostals." The enthusiasm and profound faith shown by members of these groups have caused the movement to spread rapidly and to bring new spirit to elements in the church which are still tottering from the religious crisis of recent years. Indeed, so new is the movement among Catholics that it has scarcely had time to develop its own theology and to locate itself within the Christian tradition. In his valuable introduction *The Pentecostal Movement in the Catholic Church* (Notre Dame, Ind.: Ave Maria Press, 1971) Edward D. O'Connor has observed that "the right of any group to call itself Pentecostal must be measured by its faithfulness to the scriptural doctrine on the Holy Spirit and to his actual inspiration" (pp. 31-32). In my opinion one great challenge now facing Catholic Pentecostals involves their willingness to explore the New Testament in an honest and open effort to find biblical roots. More particularly, I see the question facing Pentecostals as this: Will they accept or reject the classic Pentecostal doctrine of a second baptism in the Spirit as distinct from, and subsequent to, their initial Christian baptism?

Fortunately, two good books have appeared which should help Catholic Pentecostals in answering this question. Frederick Dale Bruner describes his work *A Theology of the Holy Spirit. The Pentecostal Experience and the New Testament Witness* (Grand Rapids, Mich.: Eerdmans, 1970) as an essay in systematic theology, but he relies very heavily on New Testament exegesis. More directly exegetical is James D. G. Dunn's *Baptism in the Holy Spirit* (Studies in Biblical Theology, 2nd series 15, Naperville, Ill.: Allenson, 1970), a detailed examination of the New Testament evidence for the Pentecostal teaching of second baptism. Both are revisions of doctoral dissertations. Bruner, now of Union Seminary in the Philippines, completed his thesis at Hamburg while Dunn, now at Durham (UK), wrote his at Clare College, Cambridge. For Catholics and other traditional Christians now becoming heavily involved in various forms of Pentecostalism these two studies provide a valuable warning that what can parade as biblical fundamentalism is often in the last analysis very foreign to the Bible. Furthermore, (and this is far more important) they provide encouragement for Christians to explore the mystery of the Spirit and serve to emphasize the profound implications of baptism for our entire Christian life.

The Pentecostal Thesis

The distinctive teaching of the "classic" Pentecostal movement involves the experience, evidence and power of what Pentecostals call the "baptism in the Holy Spirit." Bruner describes the center of Pentecostal theology in this way: It is the experience of the Holy Spirit, especially in the post-conversion filling of the Holy Spirit, as evidenced initially by speaking in other tongues, through fulfilling the conditions of absolute obedience and faith (p. 57). This baptism in the Holy Spirit is a powerful and individual spiritual experience patterned after the reception of the

Holy Spirit described in Acts 2. Any historical sketch of Pentecostalism would have to include mention of John Wesley, American revivalism, and the "holiness movement." Both classic Pentecostalism and its neo-Pentecostal offshoots claim that the power for spiritual life in the individual and in the church is to be found in baptism in the Spirit with its charismatic manifestations.

While the Spirit has baptized every believer into Christ, Pentecostals maintain that Christ has not yet baptized every believer into the Spirit; so there is need for a second baptism distinct from, and subsequent to, the first. The doctrine is usually based exegetically on the baptism of Jesus (Mk 1:9-11 and parallels), Pentecost (Acts 2), the second baptism at Samaria (Acts 8:4-25), Paul's conversion (Acts 9:1-19), Cornelius' conversion (Acts 10-11), and the baptism of the Ephesian disciples (Acts 19:1-7).

Pentecostals feel that this baptism in the Spirit is necessary because it adds to initial or converting faith the dwelling of the Spirit and, hence, power for service along with the gifts of the Spirit. For Pentecostals the initial evidence that one has been baptized in the Spirit is speaking in tongues as the disciples did in Acts 2:4. Pentecost thus becomes a pattern for all Christians at all times. Just as the members of Cornelius' household (Acts 10:45-46) and the disciples at Ephesus (Acts 19:6) shared this experience, so can Christians of our own day. Other gifts which are valued highly among Pentecostals are healing, prophecy and the interpretation of tongues. In describing various manifestations of these gifts Bruner observes that the Pentecostal assembly is 1 Cor 12—14 come alive.

At the very outset of his work, Dunn also states the distinctive theological stance underlying classic Pentecostalism: Baptism in the Holy Spirit is a second Pentecostal experience distinct from, and subsequent to, conversion-initiation. This second baptism gives power for witness. Speaking in tongues is the necessary and inevitable evidence of baptism in the Holy Spirit, and so it is only fitting that the spiritual gifts listed in 1 Cor 12:8-10 be manifested when Pentecostal Christians meet for worship.

The Baptism of Jesus by John

Bruner sees the contrast drawn in Mk 1:8 between John's baptism and the promised baptism with the Holy Spirit as an indication that through the power of Christ's name baptism could no longer merely be baptism in water. Indeed, in John's baptism of Jesus at the Jordan (Mk 1:9-11) the connection between baptism and the coming of the Spirit is made particularly vivid by the word "immediately." Baptism in water and the descent of the Spirit are one. Spiritual baptism has been formed and inaugurated in the person of its elect dispenser—Jesus Christ. For Bruner, the baptism of Jesus corresponds with the church's baptism since it is in water, is accompanied immediately with the Spirit, and means sonship.

Dunn's analysis here is quite different. He prefers to begin from Q (the source used by Mt and Lk): "He will baptize you with the Holy Spirit and fire (Mt 3:11 and Lk 3:16)." While John's baptism in water prepares for the eschatological baptism, the coming baptism is not necessarily envisioned as a form of water-baptism; "baptism" is merely a metaphor to heighten the contrast with John's baptism. Even though Mark omits mention of "fire" and all talk of judgment, he is still careful not to conflate Spirit-baptism with water-baptism. Where Pentecostals see the baptism of Jesus (Mt 3:13-17; Mk 1:9-11; Lk 3:21-22; Jn 1:29-34) in the Jordan as proving the need for an additional blessing to equip one with power for his mission, sacramentalists tend to view the event as the fusion of water-baptism and the promised Spirit-baptism. Against the Pentecostals Dunn argues that the experience of Jesus is a unique moment in salvation-history in which the decisive change in the ages from old to new is effected by the descent of the Spirit. At the same time, he admits that Jesus' anointing with the Spirit did also equip him for his messianic ministry of healing and teaching. Against the sacramentalists he states that the baptism of John is distinct from, and only preliminary to, the descent of the Spirit. In the final analysis the bestowal of the Spirit is entirely the action of the Father and cannot be equated with baptism in water.

Acts of the Apostles

Since Acts looms so large in the Pentecostal thesis, Bruner leads us through this book in an effort to find answers to these questions: "Does Pentecostalism rightly or wrongly understand Luke, accurately or mistakenly interpret him, properly or improperly apply him?" (p. 153). In the first few verses of Acts the Holy Spirit is seen as Jesus' way of working in his church (1:1-2), and the church is said to receive the Spirit freely and inclusively as a promise (1:4-5). At Pentecost the Spirit is clearly a free gift from God filling each one of the disciples (2:3-4); the means by which others are to receive this gift are Christian preaching (2:14-36) and baptism (2:37-39). According to Luke, baptism in the name of Jesus Christ includes both the forgiveness of sin and the reception of the Spirit (2:38); in other words, baptism is visible evidence for the forgiveness of sins and the coordinate gift of the Spirit. The Holy Spirit is a free gift, and neither prayer (4:31) nor obedience (5:32) can be seen as conditions which compel this gift. Dunn's treatment of Pentecost stresses that what the experience of the Jordan was for Jesus, Pentecost was for the disciples. Pentecost is the new beginning, the inauguration of the new age, the age of the Spirit. Jesus, having exhausted the fire kindled upon him (Lk 12:49-50), now baptizes with the Holy Spirit (Acts 1:5). Since the coming of the Spirit at Pentecost begins the age of the church and since the event of Pentecost is thus a unique step in the Lukan scheme of salvation-history, it cannot serve to found the Pentecostal belief in a secondary baptism empowering for mission: "The fact is that the phrase 'baptism in the Spirit' is never directly associated with the promise of power, but it always associated with entry into the messianic age or the Body of Christ (p. 54)."

In Acts 8 we come upon the curious story of the Samaritans who have believed and been baptized but do not receive the Holy Spirit until some time later. Bruner theorizes that God withheld the gift of the Spirit until the leading apostles Peter and John could see with their own eyes that the gift of the Spirit was free and for all—not merely for Jews. At any rate, what Luke wants to emphasize by the incident is that the coming of the Spirit completes baptism and belongs properly to it. Therefore, the story presupposes the union of initiatory baptism and the Spirit rather than their separation. Bruner also notes that there is no mention of the Samaritans' speaking in tongues upon receiving the Spirit, and he sees Simon's desire for spiritual power offensive to Peter precisely because it suggests that God's gift can be obtained by human means. Dunn also feels that Luke intends to show that the Samaritans' first response was defective. To the Samaritans Philip's message may have meant the appearance of their own expected Messiah and his kingdom, and their conversion could have had more of the emotional herd-instinct about it than Christian commitment. The fact that Simon the magician could accept the form of baptism while remaining so dense toward its meaning underscores this point. The second baptism is merely a means to rectify a mistake. Since the Samaritans had not received the Spirit, their baptism and faith could not have been genuine.

The fact that Paul was baptized in the Spirit three days after his experience on the road to Damascus (Acts 9, 22, 26) does not impress Dunn as a valid argument for the Pentecostal thesis. Rather, several factors indicate that Paul's three-day experience was a unity, a crisis-experience extending over three days from the Damascus road to his baptism. First, according to Acts 22:16 Paul still had to take the major step toward commitment and forgiveness even after his experience on the road. Secondly, Paul does not distinguish between the commissioning on the Damascus road (Acts 26:12-18) and that which he received through Ananias (Acts 9:15; 22:12-16). Finally, his three-day blindness probably is meant to recall Jesus' three days in the tomb and to symbolize his transition from spiritual blindness to enlightenment. On this matter, Bruner notes that in Acts 9:17-19 baptism and the reception of the Spirit are so synonymous as to be identical and so it is not even necessary to mention the Spirit in 22:16.

In the Cornelius episode (Acts 10—11) the gift of the Holy Spirit is clearly conversion rather than any subsequent experience. As at Pentecost, the gift of tongues is totally unsought, unexpected and undemanded. In fact, so close are the parallels in Acts 10:44-48 and 11:13-18 with Acts 2 that Bruner is led to see the event as a kind of Gentile Pentecost. Peter in Acts 10:47 feels obliged to baptize Cornelius and his household in water because the gift of the Holy Spirit without baptism was as unthinkable to the church as baptism without the gift of the Holy Spirit. Dunn notes that, however well disposed Cornelius was before, what made him a Christian and brought him into the salvation of the new age was belief in Jesus Christ and the gift of the Holy Spirit. In this incident baptism in the Spirit is God's act of acceptance (of forgiveness, cleansing and salvation), and not something separate from and beyond that which made Cornelius a Christian.

In Paul's questions to the Ephesian disciples ("Did you receive the Holy Spirit when you believed?" "Into what then were you baptized?" Acts 19:2-3) Bruner feels there are almost classic statements of how the Holy Spirit comes and of the union in the apostolic consciousness of faith, baptism and the gift of the Holy Spirit. Because they have been baptized into John's baptism only, Paul must begin with what is fundamental for Christian life—believing in Jesus and consequent Christian baptism. Dunn argues that the unusual description of the Ephesian disciples ("some disciples" without the article) deliberately indicates their lack of formal relation to the church at Ephesus. Furthermore, since the absence of the Spirit meant that one had not yet begun Christian life, Paul is asking whether or not the Ephesian disciples are really Christians. When he finds they are not, he remedies the situation in a ceremony consisting of baptism, the laying on of hands and the reception of the Spirit.

Throughout Acts, Bruner maintains, the fundamental gift of the Spirit comes but once in Christ and does not need any filling out or improvement. In neither Acts 2, 8, 10 nor 19—the standard texts for a second baptism—is there any evidence of the Spirit's first and partial entry followed by his second and personal reception. All these texts teach one entry of the Spirit. Therefore, Bruner can conclude that classic Pentecostalism wrongly understands Luke, mistakenly interprets him and improperly applies him. Dunn summarizes his discussion of Acts by observing that the one thing which makes a man a Christian is the gift of the Spirit and that this gift comes in conversion. Dunn also distinguishes the Spirit from water-baptism: Faith reaches out to God in and through water-baptism while God reaches out to man and meets that faith in and through his Spirit.

Other Evidence

A large part of Bruner's work is devoted to a systematic survey of the "way of the Holy Spirit according to the New Testament" and its consequences for Pentecostal doctrine. Here the focus is mainly on Paul's teaching with some attention also paid to John. While the end-product is a systematic understanding, the method by which this is gained is thoroughly exegetical. Pentecostalism, according to Bruner, makes the mastery of sin a condition for receiving the grace of the Holy Spirit and thereby perverts the Pauline perspective of grace as the condition for mastering sin. The "Spirit of life" comes in Christ Jesus (Gal 3:14), and not as a second experience independent of, or in addition, to Jesus Christ. The Pentecostal distinction between Christians and Spirit-filled Christians contradicts Paul's clear teaching in Colossians that baptized Christians have already found spiritual fulfillment in Christ and that there is no need for a second transformation to live, serve, work and witness as a Christian. By requiring speaking in tongues as the initial evidence and ultimate condition of God's full gift, classic Pentecostalism deserves all the warnings which Paul lays upon the circumcision party in Gal 5:2-12. For Paul the believer receives everything God has to give through Christ in faith. To require a supplement to faith or a condition for fullness before God is to repeat the oldest of Christian heresies and to deny the power of Christ.

Since the zeal of the ancient Corinthians was deflecting them from (or beyond) Christocentricity and since there are echoes of this tendency in contemporary Pentecostalism, Bruner feels it necessary to devote an entire chapter to 1 Cor 12—14 and 2 Cor 10—13. Paul understands the work of the Spirit to be the honoring of Jesus Christ and the work of the spiritually gifted to be the service of the body of Christ (1 Cor 12). While Paul does not deny that speaking in tongues is a charism, he would like to see it subordinated to the larger concerns of the church (1 Cor 14:1-19) and so finds prophecy or witness to be preferable (1 Cor 14:20-25). In 2 Cor 10 — 13 the most prominent features of "Corinthianism" — pride of power, "fuller" gospel, unusual interest in visions and higher experiences, and the quest for oral evidence — seem to Bruner to correspond to what is most characteristic of 20th century Pentecostalism. To the Corinthians Paul can only answer that their "super-apostles" (2 Cor 11:5) are really "sham-apostles" (2 Cor 11:13). Unlike these false apostles Paul boasts in his sufferings and weakness because God's power "is made perfect in weakness" (2 Cor 12:9).

In his treatment of the other New Testament writings Dunn begins by examining in chronological order those Pauline passages which deal with conversion-initiation. In the earliest letters (1 and 2 Thes, Gal) the correlatives Spirit and faith are the dominant themes. Becoming a Christian is essentially a matter of receiving the Spirit, and the Spirit is received by the exercise of faith which the Christian message stirs up (Gal 3:2). The rite of water-baptism merely complements the more important dimension of faith. Nowhere is there any talk of the subsequent coming of the Holy Spirit. In 1 and 2 Cor the Spirit is the essence of the new covenant in its application to man. So dominant is this theme that in every baptismal context the gift of the Spirit is pre-eminent to the point that little, if anything, is said about the accompanying rite. In Rom Paul relates baptism explicitly to the Christian's burial with Christ (6:4). Dunn maintains that there is a clear distinction between the metaphor of "being baptized" and the rite of baptism (6:3-4). Baptism is basically commitment to the Risen Lord (6:4; 10:9-17), and Christ is experienced through the Spirit (8:9-11). The distinction between the cleansing action of the Spirit and the rite of baptism is maintained throughout Dunn's investigation of the later Pauline and post-Pauline materials. Finally, the "washing of regeneration" and the "renewal in the Holy Spirit" in Tit 3:5 are seen as virtually synonymous and not at all expressive of two distinct experiences.

In Jn the Paraclete passages envision a later bestowal of the Spirit following Jesus' final return to the Father after his various appearances to the disciples. But in Jn 20:22 the disciples are said to receive the Spirit from the Risen Lord. Therefore, John may well have considered that baptism in the Spirit was a second and distinct work of the Spirit in the experiences of the first disciples. While admitting that two outpourings of the Spirit may be implied, Dunn maintains that the chronological sequence of events in the lives of the apostles is unique and unrepeatable. Since their experiences were determined by utterly unique events (the coming of the Word, his being lifted up on the cross, the sending of the "other Paraclete"), they cannot serve as the pattern for the regular experience of conversion and Christian growth after Pentecost. In Jn 3:5 ("unless one is born of water and the

Spirit, he cannot enter the kingdom of God") water and baptism are neither contrasted nor equated, but rather they are coordinated: Both are means of effecting birth "from above." Dunn feels that John may be arguing here against the disciples of the Baptist who still were over-valuing John's baptism or even against Christians who over-valued the sacramental rite. In 1 Jn both the anointing mentioned in 2:20 and 27 and seed of 3:9 refer to the Spirit using the proclamation and teaching of the Gospel. There are no grounds for saying that John is thinking of an activity of the Spirit at baptism. On the other hand, the water and blood of 5:6 and 8 designate the key events (baptism and death?) in the incarnate ministry of Jesus and do not refer to the sacraments.

Heb 6:4-5 describes the conversion experience ("tasting") in both its inward and outward aspects: The gift and the Spirit are experienced in the heart while the word and the powers are heard and seen. The same dynamic underlies Heb 10:22: The heart "sprinkled clean from an evil conscience" is the inward, hidden aspect of man; the body "washed with pure water" is the outward, visible aspect. Dunn feels that 1 Pet 3:21 which characterizes baptism as a water-rite cleansing the body and as an expression of man's repentance and/or faith to God is the nearest approach to a definition of baptism that the New Testament affords. For Dunn, baptism is the means by which man comes to God; God comes to man through the word of preaching, and the meeting takes place by the sanctifying power of the Spirit (1 Pet 1:23).

Evaluations

As an essay in systematic theology based solidly on Scripture Bruner's work is very successful. Among the particularly valuable features in the volume are the analysis of representative Pentecostal documents, the effort to place the movement within a historical setting, and the thirty-four pages of bibliographical information. Furthermore, his use of the New Testament is constructive and well-based on the best in modern biblical scholarship. Clarity and sharp logic mark Dunn's monograph. The scope of his work is more limited than Bruner's and so it may not be as helpful in introducing the reader to the Pentecostal use of Scripture. On the other hand, Dunn seems far more at home in biblical exegesis. Usually his analysis is fresher and more perceptive than Bruner's somewhat conventional interpretation.

A description of points at which the two authors differ in interpreting Mk and Acts may bring out this last judgment more decisively. Bruner sees Jesus' baptism in water and the Spirit as the prototype of Christian baptism and tends to emphasize the "typical" character of Pentecost. Dunn sees no relation at all between John's baptism of Jesus in the Jordan and Christian baptism. What is significant is the descent of the Holy Spirit, and this is wholly distinct from the rite in the Jordan. Furthermore, Dunn sees Pentecost as initiating a totally new epoch in the history of salvation. Therefore, the primary meaning of Pentecost is found in its unique, once for all character; its significance as a model for religious experience can only be secondary. In trying to explain why the baptism of the Samaritans in Acts 8 is defective, Bruner chooses to see it as a lesson for the leading apostles that God's gift is meant for all people while Dunn claims that the initial commitment was merely emotional and needed deepening. Both seem to be guessing here. While Bruner appears willing to admit that the Ephesian disciples of Acts 19 were somehow Christians, Dunn maintains they could not have been before receiving the Holy Spirit.

Both authors have devoted a great deal of space and effort to Acts because it is from Acts that Pentecostals draw most of their biblical ammunition and because the role of the Spirit is so central in Acts. Both have shown how important receiving the Spirit and the subsequent charismatic evidences are in Luke's theology. These emphases raise serious questions for New Testament scholars and theologians: How do the people in Acts know they have received the

Holy Spirit if not through charismatic manifestation? Why did Luke, writing comparatively late in the 1st century, feel the need to emphasize speaking in tongues as a charismatic gift long after Paul had deliberately de-emphasized this gift? How valid is it to classify Luke as a representative of early catholicism in the light of his doctrine of the Spirit?

When the two authors come to Paul and the other New Testament writings, their aims and methods diverge sharply. Bruner as a systematic theologian studies Paul and John together in the hope of deducing a biblical doctrine of the Spirit while Dunn retains the strictly exegetical format. It is to Bruner's credit that he does let the individual texts speak for themselves and that he is careful to use good secondary sources. Dunn does not limit himself to Paul and John and so puts much more information at the disposal of anyone who would try to develop his own systematic doctrine of the Holy Spirit in the New Testament. If one were to summarize the basic themes of the two presentations, one could say that Bruner is especially concerned with the free or "gift" character of the Spirit in the New Testament while Dunn wants to emphasize that the essence of New Testament Christianity was an experience of receiving the Spirit.

The only general criticism of Bruner's work which we have to offer at this point involves his excessive stress on the free or unmerited nature of the gift of the Spirit. This is repeated so often that one begins to suspect that Bruner may be more evangelical than biblical here. We tend to agree with Dunn's excellent summary of the New Testament teaching on baptism: "Faith demands baptism as its expression; Baptism demands faith for its validity. The gift of the Spirit presupposes faith as its condition; Faith is shown to be genuine only by the gift of the Spirit" (p. 228). This last statement leads us into our major criticism of Dunn's study. His insistence on rigidly distinguishing the reception of the Spirit from the external rite of baptism tends to confuse even the attentive reader. Throughout the book one keeps asking Dunn whether he sees any real need to undergo the rite of water-baptism at all. At some points, one suspects

Dunn would reply that only the Spirit is essential (not as unorthodox a doctrine as it might first sound; recall the "baptism of desire" and the "baptism of blood") while at other points he is satisfied to call water-baptism a complement to faith.

At times, this insistence even mars his exegesis. Perhaps my own sacramentalism is showing here, but I found his determination to describe so many allusions to water-baptism as "metaphors" (as if this somehow lessens their importance) very strained and artificial. Surely the reception of the Spirit is the essence of baptism, but Paul's frequent allusions to the water-rite indicates his high esteem for it. Furthermore, I do not feel that Bultmann's excision of "water and" in Jn 3:5 is "wholly unwarranted." Rather I would agree with Bultmann that this phrase and 6:51b-58 have been added to the Gospel by the ecclesiastical redactor (or some such figure). The phrase is not at all developed in the passage and serves only to confuse the discourse. Dunn seems to have been led by his fixed determination that Paul and John must be distinguishing between rite and Spirit as rigidly as he himself sometimes does. The matter really only comes clear at the end (p. 227) where Dunn explicitly rejects any separation between faith and baptism.

Dunn's (and to a lesser extent, Bruner's) use of the terms "Pentecostal" and "Sacramentalist" as deviations from the correct *via media* may strike some as caricatures. Many who have been "baptized in the Spirit" are willing to view their experience as the unique and decisive event in their lives and are not especially interested in distinguishing it from conversion-initiation or in taking upon themselves the burden of Pentecostal theology. On the other hand, I cannot imagine any modern sacramental theologian who would not see rite as the external witness to an internal experience much as Dunn does and who would not also emphasize very strongly the importance of the the recipient's attitude. Dunn really seems to be arguing against strictly *ex opere operato* magical thought-patterns when he defines himself over against sacramentalism.

As we said at the outset, these thorough studies by Bruner and Dunn provide both warning and encouragement to Catholic Pentecostals. The classic Pentecostal doctrine of baptism in the Spirit as distinct from, and subsequent to, conversion-initiation is simply not in accord with the New Testament evidence. This is clear. Yet both books prove the central importance of experiencing the Holy Spirit in New Testament thought and urge us to probe this phenomenon in our own lives. If Catholic Pentecostals will avoid the traps of classic Pentecostal theology and turn their attention to more fruitful areas of investigation, we can expect truly wonderful spiritual and theological growth.

3. THE "EARLY CATHOLIC" WRITINGS OF THE NEW TESTAMENT: THE CHURCH ADJUSTING TO WORLD-HISTORY

Among the most important contributions gained from the critical study of the Bible has been the recognition that there are varieties of Christianity within the NT itself. We have learned that Palestinian, Hellenistic, Johannine, and Pauline Christianity differ in theological expression and church structure. "Early catholicism" had previously been a term employed by church historians to describe that form of Christianity which blossomed in the second century under the influence of the Roman church. As such, it was marked by the monarchical episcopate, the notion of the church as the instrument of salvation, total loss of eschatological perspective, the canon of scripture as *regula fidei*, great emphasis on sacraments, and a clear delineation between orthodoxy and heresy. Recently, however, biblical scholars have come to see that the roots of early catholicism are to be found in certain books of the NT: Luke-Acts, 1 and 2 Timothy, Titus, Ephesians, Jude, and 2 Peter.

Ernst Käsemann sees early catholicism as an attempt to

control the ferment of enthusiasm rampant in the Pauline communities after the interventions of Paul himself had met with practical failure.[1] While the theology of early catholicism depends on Paul to a great extent, from a practical standpoint the church in Asia Minor toward the end of the first century grasped at those forms of church government which had stood the test in Jewish Christianity. But these practical measures produced some sharp contrasts with genuine Pauline theological perspectives. Eschatological expectation was pushed into the distant future or disappeared altogether. The world-pervading church was seen as the kingdom of God on earth and became the possessor of truth and mother of the faithful. There was great emphasis on cult apart from everyday life and on sacramentally guaranteed office. The perspective of salvation-history and missionary activity to spread Christianity throughout the world became increasingly important. Finally, adherence to moral standards and uniform behavior replaced Paul's emphasis on discerning the spirits.

Besides comparing it with Pauline thought, another effective way to clarify our subject is to list its characteristics. In the NT early catholicism is marked by the traces of, or tendencies toward, hierarchical rather than charismatic ministry, development of the monarchical episcopate, objectification of the kerygma and emphasis on a strictly formulated rule of faith, stress on orthodoxy and sound doctrine, moralization of faith and conception of the gospel as the "new Law," faith as objective and static, the principle of apostolic succession and transmitted authority, the distinction between clergy and laity, an authoritative interpretation of Scripture, sacramentalism, the formulation of natural theology, a concern for ecclesiastical unity and con-

---

[1]E. Käsemann, "Paulus und der Frühkatholizismus," *ZTK* 60 (1963) 75-89, ET in *New Testament Questions of Today* (Philadelphia: Fortress, 1969) 236-51. A full discussion of Käsemann's views can be found in my articles, "Ernst Käsemann on the Church in the New Testament," *HeyJ* 12 (1971) 246-57, 367-78. For a valuable history of the term *Frühkatholizismus* see now K.H. Neufeld, " 'Frühkatholizismus' — Idee und Begriff," *ZKT* 94 (1972) 1-28.

solidation, and an interest in collecting apostolic documents.[2]

Up to this point we have presented a list of NT writings and a list of tendencies formulated in a somewhat abstract manner. In this article we will try to provide a solid textual foundation for the elements of early catholicism in the NT. Rather than allowing ourselves to be guided by our preliminary descriptions, we will attempt to let the texts themselves speak and to derive our categories from them. We want to find answers to the following questions: What description emerges from studying Luke-Acts, Pastorals, Ephesians, Jude, and 2 Peter all together? Can we rightfully place these NT writings under a single heading and maintain that they are the product of a distinct movement in first-century Christianity?

Luke-Acts

Since Luke's Gospel purports to be a history of Jesus' life (1:1-4), we should not expect to find many distinctively "early catholic" features here. Yet there are some matters which deserve mention. Most important of all is the replacement of eschatological expectation by a salvation-history perspective. While Luke does take over apocalyptic images from the tradition, the imminence of the end ceases to play a vital role in his thought. In the apocalyptic tradition the outpouring of the Spirit is a sign of the eschaton, but in Luke (4:1, 14 and 21) Jesus in his ministry is already the unique bearer of the Spirit. The emphasis on patience (8:15; 21:19) suggests adjustment to an indefinite period of persecution. John the Baptist is no longer the apocalyptic forerunner but is relegated to the period of Israel (16:16). Discussion about the exact time of the eschaton is shut off (17:20-21; 19:11-27; 21:7-9).

---

[2]The list is from J. H. Elliott, "A Catholic Gospel: Reflections on 'Early Catholicism' in the New Testament," *CBQ* 31 (1969) 214.

In contrast with the "this age"/"age to come" apocalyptic scheme of history that most NT writers have taken over from Judaism, Luke presents a more nuanced history of salvation which distinguishes the period of Israel (16:16), the period of Jesus' ministry (4:16 ff.) and the time of the church after the ascension with the parousia as the end of saving-history.[3] Within this framework Luke tries to secure Jesus' place (and, by implication, the church's) in Roman history by stressing that Jesus was crucified by the Jews on a religious matter rather than by the Romans on a political charge. 13:31-35 states that Jesus died as a prophet rather than as a political insurgent. The political charge levelled by the Jews against Jesus is a lie (20:20 and 23:2). In 23:24-25 Pilate does not condemn Jesus; he merely hands him over to the Jews.

According to Luke's salvation-history perspective the time of Jesus is a unique period of the past, and so there is no need for Luke to project the offices and institutions of the church back into the life of Jesus. There is, however, one important exception: In 6:13 the Twelve are called "apostles." This equation between the Twelve and the apostles will be very significant in Acts. Also, in 8:3 the women who minister (*diēkonoun*) to Jesus may be assimilated to the deaconesses of Luke's church, and in 2:36-38 the figure of Anna may have some connection with the order of widows (1 Tim 5:3-16 and possibly Acts 6:1 and 9:39).

While Luke clearly had access to older traditions when he composed Acts around A.D. 100, he was also concerned with speaking to people of his own time and did so in some of the categories of early catholicism. When the apostles ask the risen Lord about the coming kingdom, they are told that the exact time is a divine decision and that now they, upon receiving the Spirit, are to spread Christianity to the ends of the earth (Acts 1:6-8). In 2:17 the "last days" foreseen by Joel are equated with the outpouring of the Holy Spirit at Pentecost. Thus the heightened eschatological conscious-

[3]H. Conzelmann, *The Theology of Saint Luke* (London: Faber, 1960).

ness witnessed in Mark and Paul is being replaced by the doctrines of the Holy Spirit, the church, and history as the progress of the gospel.

In many places Luke provides his own theological summaries which emphasize unity as characteristic of the earliest community: 1:14 "with one accord"; 2:44 "And all who believed were together and had all things in common"; 4:32-35 where community of goods symbolizes unity in belief; and so forth. Thus the apostolic age is seen as an ideal and privileged period marked by idyllic unity. This perspective even leads Luke to gloss over the real division between the Hebrews and the Hellenists echoed in Acts 6:1-7. Furthermore, the discourses in the early sections of Acts (2:14-42; 3:12-26; 4:24-30; 5:30-32; 10:34-43; 13:16-41) are all built on the same basic pattern: The OT prophecies have been fulfilled; Jesus the Messiah has been born, crucified, and buried; God raised him from the dead and exalted him to his right hand; the Spirit has been sent; the Messiah will return in judgment; therefore repent and be baptized. No matter who the speaker is, the speech is the same. Clearly Luke wants to show what preaching should be and to demonstrate the "one faith" of the earliest church. The pattern illustrates a tendency toward a fixed creed with definite elements.

While there is surprisingly little interest in the Eucharist (2:42, 46; 20:7, 11; Does the "breaking of bread" mean the Eucharist?), there is a great deal of interest in baptism. Throughout Acts (2:38; 8:14-24, 37; 9:18; 10:47-48; 16:15, 33; 18:8; 19:1-7) Luke makes a conscious effort to show that baptism is the proper expression of faith and that the gift of the Spirit and baptism are inseparable.[4] Moreover, for Luke (unlike Paul!) an apostle is one who accompanied Jesus in his earthly ministry (1:21-22; 4:13). Since the apostles are equated with the Twelve, the traditional description of Paul as an apostle (14:4, 14) causes some embarrassment and

[4]See my article "Baptism in the Spirit: A Review Article," *Chicago Studies* 11 (1972) 31-44.

leads Luke to assimilate Paul to the Twelve (9:15-17). The Twelve at Jerusalem exercise an almost hierarchical function. Peter is spokesman for the Holy Spirit (5:1-11). The second baptism at Samaria suggests that the Holy Spirit is given only in conjunction with the authorization of the Twelve (8:14-19). Paul's "going-up" to Jerusalem soon after his conversion (9:23-30) serves to relate his mission to the apostolic college right from the start. The Jerusalem church sends Barnabas to Antioch to check on the developing Gentile mission (11:22-24). The "council" of Jerusalem (15:1-35) is depicted as ratifying Paul's gospel and as making a decision for the whole church. Aberrant forms of belief (Apollos in 18:24-28 and the disciples at Ephesus in 19:1-7) are incorporated into the mainstream. Finally, while it is difficult to discover a clear system of church offices in Acts, Luke does seem far more interested than Paul in ecclesiastical offices and the ritual transmission of authority. There are apostles (=the Twelve), the Seven in 6:1-6 (are they properly called "deacons"?), and elders in 14:23; 15:4; 20:17 and 21:18. The elders of Ephesus are addressed as *episkopoi* in 20:28. James in 21:18 appears to function as the resident bishop of Jerusalem. In 6:6 the authority of the Twelve is transmitted to the Seven by the imposition of hands, and in 13:3 the church leaders at Antioch lay hands on Paul and Barnabas to make them apostolic founders.

Even the figure of Paul in Acts has been influenced by the perspectives of early catholicism.[5] Our control here, of course, is the figure of Paul as seen in the undoubtedly authentic Pauline epistles (1 Thes, Gal, Rom, 1 and 2 Cor, Phil, Phlm). In 17:22-31 Paul adapts the Christian kerygma to the needs of the Gentiles in the form of natural or philosophical theology. He appears as the skilled Hellenistic orator (17:22, 28; see also 26:1-23). He is depicted as living the life of an observant Jew even after his conversion (21:24; 22:3,

---

[5]P. Vielhauer, "On the 'Paulinism' of Acts," *Studies in Luke-Acts. Essays presented in honor of Paul Schubert* (ed. L. E. Keck and J. L. Martyn; Nashville: Abingdon, 1966) 33-50.

17; 23:6; 24:14; 26:5). Also, he is everywhere absolved by the Roman authorities as innocent of any crime; opposition to Paul stems from the Jews alone and depends on a purely religious disagreement (25:19). This portrait of Paul allows Luke to get across the points that Christianity is a form of Judaism and thus a *religio licita*, and the Roman authorities have absolutely nothing to fear from the Christians. This outlook means that the church no longer expects an immediate end and is now adjusting itself to life as an element in world-history.

Pastorals

Because they are addressed to pastors and are largely concerned with their duties, 1 and 2 Timothy along with Titus are commonly called the Pastoral Epistles. Whether they were composed by Paul himself in the later stages of his career or were written by a disciple around A.D. 100 in Paul's name is still not thoroughly determined. No one of the arguments against Pauline authorship (absence in earliest MSS, the frequency of pseudonymous authorship at the time, the Jewish-Christian gnosticism of the opponents, the strong emphasis on official ministry, the "non-Pauline" theology) is decisive. Yet all admit that the vocabulary and style are markedly different from that of the acknowledged Paulines. But even this fact can be explained in several different ways: Paul's literary style has developed; he is employing a new scribe or at least giving the scribe more freedom; a disciple has worked over Pauline fragments; a disciple is composing freely in Paul's name.[6]

Whatever decision one takes on the matter of authorship, there can be little doubt that the Pastorals present many early catholic perspectives. While eschatological expectation does function as an important element in Christian

---

[6]In antiquity pseudonymity need not mean fraud. For the many reasons underlying pseudonymous authorship see B. M. Metzger, "Literary Forgeries and Canonical Pseudepigrapha," *JBL* 91 (1972) 3-24.

faith, there is no real sense that the end is temporally close. Christ Jesus is called "our hope" in 1 Tim 1:1, but the phrase is left undeveloped. The "later times" are invoked as a period of great evil in 4:1, but the context shows that the author is merely using a literary form to talk about the present. The Lord's appearance will come "at the proper time" (6:15). 2 Tim 1:12 and 18 allude to the day of judgment, but there is no indication that this is at hand. 2 Tim 3:1 speaks of "the last days" as a period of moral crisis, but 3:5 ("Avoid such people") makes it plain that the author is referring to the present. 2 Tim 4:1 describes Christ as judge of the living and the dead; in 4:8 Paul expects his reward "on that day." Tit 2:13 ("awaiting our blessed hope, the appearing of the glory of our great God and Savior Jesus Christ") shows that eschatology remains a lively theme even though it is no longer at the center of Christian theology.

There is great emphasis in the Pastorals on faith considered as an objective deposit. Timothy is charged not to teach any different doctrine (1 Tim 1:3). The mystery of faith is something to be held (3:9). The church of God is "the pillar and bulwark of the truth" (3:15). Timothy is to be nourished on sound doctrine (1:10; 4:6; 6:3) and is to guard the deposit of faith (6:20). In 2 Tim 1:13 Paul's teaching is termed "the pattern of the sound words." The gospel message is again described as deposit and regarded as a precious trust to be guarded (1:12, 14). Timothy is instructed to entrust what he has heard to faithful men who will be able to teach others (2:2). In Tit 1:9 the *episkopos* is to hold firm to the sure word as taught so he can give instruction in sound doctrine and refute those who contradict it. Sound doctrine is the basis of all good works (2:1). The content of this sound doctrine can be glimpsed in the creedal statements and hymnic fragments cited in 1 Tim 1:15; 2:5-6; 3:16; 6:13; 2 Tim 2:8; 2:11b-13; Tit 3:4-7. These confessions hint at the tendencies toward an objective and static concept of faith, a strictly formulated rule of faith, and clear delineation between orthodoxy and heresy.[7]

[7]H. Conzelmann, *An Outline of the Theology of the New Testament* (New York: Harper & Row, 1969) 296-99.

The author of the Pastorals has specific opponents in mind. Best described as "Jewish-Christian gnostics," they teach by myth and genealogy (1 Tim 1:4), claim to be teachers of the Law (1:7), apparently restrict the number of the saved (2:1 and 4:10), forbid marriage and enjoin abstinence (4:3), and may be teetotalers (5:23). In 2 Tim 2:18 we hear that they teach that the resurrection is already past. The comparison with Jannes and Jambres (Pharaoh's magicians in the OT tradition) in 3:8 implies an interest in magic while in 3:13 they are specifically called *goētes* (="magicians"). 2 Tim 2:16; 3:9 and 3:13 suggest that "progress" was an important theme in their preaching. The Cretan opponents in Tit seem to be similar to the Ephesian opponents of 1 and 2 Tim. Again they are best described as Jewish-Christian gnostics: They belong to the circumcision party (1:10) and propagate Jewish myths (1:14); they lay down specific food laws (1:14-15); they profess to know God (1:16); they are said to be interested in speculations, genealogies, and disputes about the Law (3:9). The statement that salvation is offered to all men (2:11) may point to an exclusivist orientation in the opponents' preaching; this could be either anti-Gentile bias on the part of Jews or an elitism found among gnostics (or both!).

The author's assessment of his opponents is fiercely negative. Their teaching is branded as vain discussion (1 Tim 1:6), godless and silly myths (4:7), and the falsely-called gnosis (6:20). Their craving for controversy leads to dissension and issues in religious commercialism (6:4-5). In 2 Tim their teaching is described as disputes about words (2:14) and godless chatter (2:16). Their stupid and senseless controversies breed quarrels (2:23); their minds are corrupt, and they oppose the truth (3:8). In Tit they are empty talkers and deceivers who upset people and seek their own financial gain (1:10-11). Their minds and consciences are corrupted, and by their deeds they deny God (1:15-16). Anyone who holds such views is *hairetikos* and should be avoided (3:10).

There are elements of sacramentalism. In 1 Tim 4:14 Timothy's charism has been confirmed and mediated through the imposition of hands. He himself is not to be hasty in imposing hands on presbyters (5:22). In 2 Tim 1:6

Timothy is told to rekindle the charism that is within him "through the laying on of my hands." In Tit 3:5 baptism is termed "the washing of regeneration and renewal in the Holy Spirit."

The Pastorals place much emphasis on church offices. The definite standards laid down for the *episkopos* and *diakonos* in 1 Tim 3:1-13 necessarily lead to the clergy-lay distinction. 1 Tim 5:17-22 lists regulations for the presbyter—his salary, the procedure to be followed when he is accused of sin, and provision for evaluation prior to ordination. 1 Tim 5:3-16 suggests the existence of an officially recognized order of widows with carefully specified entrance requirements. In Tit 1:5-9 Titus is charged with the responsibility of setting up a church organization on Crete. He is to appoint presbyters and an *episkopos* (from the board of presbyters?).[8] Among the tasks of the latter is fidelity to the gospel in presenting sound doctrine and refuting error (1:9).

Finally, the Pastorals show how the church is adjusting to world-history and to its place in the secular world. The ideal is faith and a good conscience (1 Tim 1:5, 19; 3:9). Christians are to pray for kings and all in high positions so they can lead a "quiet and peaceable life, godly and respectful in every way" (2:2). External respectability is very important (3:7, 13; 5:14; 6:1). Women are to perform good deeds, be silent, and bear children (2:9-15). The moral virtues recommended for various age-groups in Tit 2:1-10 are generally the virtues recommended by philosophers to all men of the period. Christ came to raise the moral level of human life (2:11-14). An important motive for practical moral action is the respect such conduct will win from the external community (2:5, 7, 10). Christians are exhorted to be submissive to rulers and to show perfect courtesy to all men (3:1-2).

---

[8]For the historical roots of the presbyteral and episcopal/diaconal structures see R. Bultmann, *Theology of the New Testament* (London: SCM, 1955), vol. 2; also H. von Campenhausen, *Ecclesiastical Authority and Spiritual Power in the Church of the First Three Centuries* (Stanford: Stanford University, 1969).

Ephesians

Again while no single argument against the Pauline authorship of Ephesians (the very Semitic style, the use of terms such as *mystērion* and *oikonomia* in an un-Pauline fashion, the distinctive theological outlook) is absolutely decisive, the combination of all of them has convinced many modern scholars that it was composed between A.D. 80 and 100 by a disciple of Paul in Asia Minor.[9] At any rate, the letter does contain a number of what we have come to recognize as early catholic elements: the lessening of eschatological expectation, the identification of the church with the body of Christ, emphasis on church unity, the apostolic foundation of the church, and sacramentalism.

As in the other early catholic writings there are many allusions to future hope (1:14, 21; 2:7; 4:30; 5:5-6; 5:13), but a heightened eschatological consciousness is absent. Rather we have the notion of the universal mission of the church and of gradual growth toward the final consummation. In Christ the whole structure is joined together and grows into a holy temple (2:21). The goal is to attain "to the unity of the faith and of the knowledge of the Son of God, to mature manhood, to the measure of the stature of the fullness of Christ" (4:13). "Bodily growth" is mentioned in 4:16. The recommendation of discipline and instruction for the young (6:4) suggests a long-term view where the end is no longer seen as imminent. At the same time, there is an effort to describe God's action in history as a plan (1:10; 3:9) and as a purpose (1:9; 3:11).

Following the lead of Colossians 1:18, 24,[10] the author of Ephesians clearly identifies the church with the body of Christ: "the church which is his body" (1:22-23).[11] Christ has

[9] P. Feine, J. Behm, and W.G. Kümmel, *Introduction to the New Testament* (Nashville: Abingdon, 1966) 251-56. At least it is certain that it was not intended solely (if at all) for the Ephesians.

[10] C. L. Mitton, *The Epistle to the Ephesians* (Oxford: Clarendon, 1951).

[11] For the background of the concept consult E. Lohse, *Colossians and Philemon* (Hermeneia; Philadelphia: Fortress 1971) 52-56. See the masterful article of J. Gnilka, "Das Kirchenmodell des Epheserbriefes," *BZ* 15 (1971) 161-84.

reconciled us to God "in one body through the cross" (2:16). In Christ the Gentiles along with the people of Israel have become members of the same body (3:6). There is one body and one Spirit (4:4). The task and goal of ecclesiastical ministry is "building up the body of Christ" (4:12). Christ is the head to whom the whole body is joined (4:15-16). The motive for truthfulness and honesty is the fact that "we are members one of another" (4:25). Christ is the head of the church, his body, and its savior (5:23). The church is the object of his love, and he gave himself up for it (5:25). We who belong to Christ's church are members of Christ's body (5:29-30). The real meaning of Gen 2:24 ("the two shall become one") has been revealed in the union of Christ with his church (5:32).

The privileges accorded to Christ are also given to his body. The members were chosen before the foundation of the world and destined to be God's sons through Jesus Christ (1:4-5). God has made us alive with Christ, raised us up with him and made us sit with him in the heavenly places (2:5-6). It is through the church that the principalities and powers who inhabit the heavenly places may come to know the manifold wisdom of God (3:10). In 3:21 God is said to show forth his glory in the church and in Christ Jesus; note that the church is placed in synonymous parallelism with Christ. Christians are being drawn "to mature manhood, to the measure of the stature of the fullness of Christ" (4:13).

Unity between Jewish-Christians and Gentile-Christians—a central theme in the letter—is based on the mystery of God's will that in the fullness of time all things should be united in Christ (1:9-10). Christ has broken down the wall of hostility between Jew and Gentile and has created in himself one new man (2:14-15). Jews and Gentiles are described as "inheriting together, embodied together, sharing together" (3:6). The unity of the Spirit is in the bond of peace (4:3). 4:4-6 is the classic statement of Christian unity: "one body and one Spirit . . . one hope . . . one Lord, one faith, one baptism, one God and Father of us all." The ministers of the church enable Christians to attain to the unity of faith and maturity while the sign of immaturity is to be swayed from sound doctrine (4:13-14).

The author is much concerned to show that the church has an apostolic foundation. The household of God is "built upon the foundation of the apostles and prophets" (2:20). The mystery of Christ has now been revealed "to his holy apostles and prophets by the Spirit" (3:5). Paul is *the* apostle to the Gentiles (3:8) and the one who reveals God's plan (3:9). In 4:11-12 ministry is called a gift and is concretized in the offices of apostle, prophet, evangelist, pastor, and teacher. While the first two may belong to an idealized apostolic generation, the last three clearly refer to offices in the author's community.

Baptism is described as the seal of the Spirit (1:13; 4:30) and as the guarantee of our future inheritance (1:14). The inclusion of the phrase "one baptism" in the list along with body, Spirit, hope, Lord, faith, God and Father suggests a very high esteem for the sacrament (4:5). The motivation for Christian behavior is placed in a baptismal context (4:22-23; 5:14); one is to act in a manner appropriate to his status as a baptized Christian. Baptism is even seen as a corporate act done to the church as a whole (5:26).

Finally, the word *ekklēsia* (1:22; 3:10, 21; 5:23-25, 27, 29, 32) is always used to describe the universal church rather than the local or individual church.

Jude and 2 Peter

Most scholars have come to agree that 2 Peter depends upon Jude: Almost all of Jude is repeated in 2 Pet; 2 Pet corrects Jude's chronological order of biblical history; 2 Pet softens the polemical tone by adding examples of God's mercy; 2 Pet has stricter views on quoting apocryphal books.[12] Jude is usually assigned to the late first century

---

[12]A well-balanced and clear discussion can be found in J. N. D. Kelly, *A Commentary on the Epistles of Peter and Jude* (Black's New Testament Commentaries; London: Black, 1969) 223-37.

while 2 Pet is generally placed in the early or middle of the second century. Both authors are convinced that the apostolic faith is the sure bulwark against the erroneous teachings of their opponents. 2 Pet also places an emphasis on the canon and the authoritative interpretation of Scripture.

Jude accuses his opponents of licentiousness and of denying God and Jesus Christ (4), of claiming that visionary experiences justify their conduct (8), and of pretending to be "spiritual" when in fact they are the opposite (10, 19). To insure that his people do not fall, the author lays great emphasis on the apostolic faith as the proper defense against false teaching. "The faith which was once for all delivered to the saints" (3) implies that faith is an objective body of truth, that it is by nature unalterable, and that it has been transmitted to the church. In 17 ("remember the predictions of the apostles") the apostles are clearly seen as a revered group belonging to an earlier generation. The recipients are urged to build themselves up "on your most holy faith" (20)—faith being a firm and objective foundation for Christian life.

The author of 2 Pet is concerned that the eschatological perspective will be lost altogether, and so he takes care to explain how Christ will come again. Proper moral behavior is the indispensable precondition for entering the eternal kingdom (1:10-11). The transfiguration is interpreted as proleptic confirmation that God's beloved Son will come again (1:17-19). The author seems to envisage a three-stage schema of world-history: the age before Noah ending in the Flood, the present age which will end in fire, and the new heaven and new earth established by the Day of the Lord (2:5; 3:5-7, 12-13). In answer to those who challenge the traditional eschatological doctrine, the author explains that just as the world was destroyed by the flood previously, it will be destroyed again by fire (3:5-7); that, according to Ps 90:4, human standards cannot be appropriate in estimating the speed or slowness of divine activity (3:8); that the Lord wants to allow all men to repent (3:9); and that the parousia will come unexpectedly and without warning (3:10).

The recipients are assured that their faith is of equal standing with that of the apostles (1:1). Jesus himself called the apostles to glory and excellence (1:3); with his "we" in 1:16 the author associates himself with the apostolic genera- tion and says that they were "eyewitnesses of his majesty." By placing the "apostles" parallel to the "holy prophets" of the OT he suggests that they are a venerated group who have mediated Christ's teaching to the church (3:2). Since the opponents are twisting Paul's teaching about freedom (2:19) for their own ends, the author feels obligated to show that Paul's teaching is no different from his own (3:15).

The phrase "faith of equal standing with the apostles" in 1:1 implies that the faith of later generations is the same doctrine and just as precious as apostolic faith. Faith is the basis of all other virtues (1:5). The phrase "established in the truth that you have" (1:12) suggests that the notion of a body or deposit is assumed. The term "heresy" has already acquired a very negative sense while orthodoxy is called "the way of truth" (2:1-2). Twice Christianity is described as a commandment ("the holy commandment delivered to them" 2:21; "the commandment of the Lord and Savior through your apostles" 3:2); these formulas carry the notion of faith as objective and traditional and of Christianity as a new Law.

The tendency to excise from Jude several legendary details (the angels' descent, the Michael incident, Enoch's prophecy), the rearrangement of events in their biblical and chronological order (2:4-8), and the omission of the *1 Enoch* quotation all suggest that our author has firmer ideas about the canon of Scripture than has the author of Jude. The fiction that Peter composed the work as a testament so that the recipients will "be able at any time to recall these things" means that apostolic writings were treasured and read at public services (1:15). 1:20-21 is evidence for the developing notion of the official church as the custodian of Scripture. No individual is entitled to interpret Scripture according to his personal whim. Rather the correct interpretation is that intended by the Holy Spirit who now apparently is understood as speaking through his commissioned ministers and teachers. On the other hand, the opponents twist the Scriptures to their own destruction (3:16).

Conclusion

At the beginning of our article we raised an issue which we must now address squarely and at some length. Are we justified in placing Lk-Acts, Pastorals, Ephesians, Jude, and 2 Peter under a single heading and in maintaining that they are the product of one distinct movement in early Christianity? By way of content these writings have much in common: lessening of eschatological perspective, interest in the church as an institution, concern with ecclesiastical offices, an objective rule of faith, sacramentalism, moralism, reverence for the apostles and especially for Paul, and so forth. By way of chronology many scholars place the composition of these writings in the last two decades of the first century or in the early years of the second century. By way of provenance several of the writings have explicit connections with the city of Ephesus in Asia Minor.

So it is initially tempting to see these writings as the literary product of a Pauline school or circle in Asia Minor around the turn of the century. On the basis of such indications Käsemann gives the name "early catholicism" to the final phase of the NT church "because where it appears certain basic presuppositions of the ancient church, distinguished from earliest Christianity, are also present."[13] Hans Küng proclaimed that "the Catholic principle (as to the meaning of office, the apostolic succession, ordination, teaching, etc.) is already to be found in the New Testament."[14] Both are guarded in their expression and avoid

---

[13] Käsemann, "Paulus und der Frükatholizismus," 75.

[14] H. Küng, " 'Early Catholicism' in the New Testament as a Problem in Controversial Theology," *The Council in Action* (New York: Sheed and Ward, 1963) 180.

raising the decisive question: Are these works really the product of a unitary phenomenon, of a single entity in the history-of-religions sense?

Despite their many obvious points of contact, it is probably a mistake to view these writings as the literary remains of one movement. Rather they are better seen as varied (though converging) responses to the crisis encountered when the church began to settle down and understand itself as an institution in world-history instead of as the eschatological fellowship of believers. In other words the authors met in their own ways the broad problem of the church's adjustment to world-history. "Adjustment to world-history" is an abstract and general term describing the church's efforts to stem enthusiasm, to deal with the passing of the apostolic generation (the Twelve and Paul), to come to grips with the physical growth of the church, to withstand persecution from outside the church, and so forth. John Elliott's statement is very appropriate: "Early catholic documents in the NT are inevitable results of their own historical age."[15]

The solutions offered by these authors are in the final analysis quite varied. Luke tries to show that there is salvation only within the church whose history, under divine guidance, shows a continuous progress. The Pastorals place a very heavy emphasis on organized ministry and middle-class morality as bulwarks of orthodoxy in the struggle against false teachers. The author of Ephesians stresses the identity between the body of Christ and the church; his response can be described as a theoretical ecclesiology. Finally, the authors of Jude and 2 Peter are satisfied that the apostolic faith is the sure defense against error. The point is that these basic solutions are simply not the same thing theologically, and there is really no objective warrant for adding them together and tracing them to one school or circle. Anyone wishing to do so must explain why Luke loses interest in "apostolic succession" after the beginning of

[15]Elliott, "A Catholic Gospel," 215.

Paul's mission, or why there is so little interest in "salvation-history" in the Pastorals, or why Ephesians persists in the "this age"/"age to come" eschatological scheme or why Ephesians is silent about ordination and apostolic succession, or why Jude and 2 Peter are silent about sacraments and church ministry. Finally, the hypothesis demands absolutely certain conclusions concerning the authorship and date of writings where these matters are by no means clear.

Therefore, it seems preferable to speak of "elements of early catholicism" in certain NT writings which were later assimilated and combined by the "great church" of the second century.[16] It was the genius of this second-century church to combine the various solutions presented in Lk-Acts, Pastorals, Ephesians, Jude and 2 Peter in a truly "catholic" way. It was the genius of this second-century church to recognize that "the gospel is historical because this dynamic relating of God through Jesus to man occurs through a historical man, Jesus of Nazareth, and to historical men and within the temporal and cosmic dimensions of time and space."[17]

---

[16]For a full discussion see E. Troeltsch, *The Social Teaching of the Christian Churches* (London: Macmillan 1931), 1, 39-200; J. Knox, *The Early Church and the Coming Great Church* (Nashville: Abingdon, 1955); W. Bauer, *Orthodoxy and Heresy in Earliest Christianity* (Philadelphia: Fortress, 1971).

[17]Elliott, "A Catholic Gospel," 222.

4. NEW TESTAMENT PERSPECTIVES ON THE MINISTRY OF THE WORD

The *General Catechetical Directory* places the task of the catechist within the framework of the ministry of the word. The ministry of the word is described as the communication of the message of salvation, as bringing the gospel to men (#16). It not only recalls the revelation of God's wonders in the past but also interprets human life in our own age in the light of this revelation (#11). Finding its nourishment and norm in Sacred Scripture (#14), the ministry of the word seeks "to stir up a lively faith which turns the mind to God, impels conformance with his action, leads to a living knowledge of the expressions of tradition, and speaks and manifests the true significance of the world and human existence (#16)."

The missionary preacher, the catechist, the homilist and the theologian today share in the ministry of the word. The catechist must make men's faith become living, conscious and active through the light of instruction (#17); he must lead communities and individuals to maturity in faith (#21). His duty is to introduce Christians to Scripture, church tradition, liturgy, private prayer, moral decision-making and dialogue with other faiths and cultures (##24-28). This ambitious agenda is summarized as conveying "the word of

God, as it is presented by the Church, in the language of the men to whom it is directed (#32)." In short, the catechist is called "the interpreter of the church among those who are to be instructed (#35)."

I find the emphasis on catechesis as a ministry of the word to be one of the soundest and richest elements in the entire directory. The authors have seen that the catechist is not merely an ordinary teacher but also participates in the church's ministry of teaching. Since I agree with almost everything said in the document about the ministry of the word and about catechesis as one of its several forms, this paper will not have to be negative or critical. Yet I feel there does remain a very important need to be fulfilled in regard to this topic. The term "ministry of the word" is unfamiliar to most Catholics and may leave many readers puzzled and baffled as to its meaning and importance. Many Christians may not be aware that the ministry of the word has a biblical basis which is among the most vital and significant concepts found in all of Scripture. The aim of this paper is to consider the ministry of the word in the church from a biblical perspective. In this way I hope to provide theological foundations and increased understanding for those whose privilege it is to engage in this kind of ministry.

Having stated this aim, I also feel compelled at the start to introduce some clear limits to my study lest I say nothing for having attempted to say too much. While there is much in the Old Testament of great relevance to the theme (the dynamic character of the word, the call of the prophet, etc.) I have decided to confine myself to the New Testament. I am inviting the reader to study along with me certain carefully chosen New Testament texts in an effort to formulate some significant biblical perspectives on charism as the basis of all Christian ministry, ministers of the word, the content of the word, and the dynamic which empowers the ministry of the word.

Another precision must be introduced here. The New Testament has little to say specifically about the ministry of catechesis, but it has a great deal to say about other ministries of the word such as apostleship and evangelization. This paper builds on the certainly justifiable assumption made in the directory that all of these are variant forms of the one ministry of the word. But there will be some obvious differences between the apostle's exercise of that ministry in the 1st century and the catechist's today. Surely catechists today have no obligation to repeat Paul's experience or imitate to the letter his form of ministry. The point here is a simple one: While we cannot and should not imitate all the particulars of Paul's ministry, we can still learn from it because apostleship and catechesis are both ministries of the word.

Charism as the Basis for All Christian Ministry

Those who usually identify ministry in the church with ecclesiastical ordination will be surprised at the document's insistence on catechesis as a ministry of the word. Catechesis is being understood as a teaching-preaching ministry, and that teaching-preaching ministry is apparently being grounded in Paul's teaching on charism as the basis of ministry. For Paul, charism is the concretion and individuation of God's grace and of the Holy Spirit; it is the unique way in which each member of the body of Christ is called to express himself for the upbuilding and service of the church. In the various lists of charisms in the Pauline writings (1 Cor 12:28; Rom 12:6-8; Eph 4:11) teaching is cited along with apostleship, prophecy, miracle-working, healing, and administration as an example of a sphere in which the Christian can build up the body of Christ.

Since the catechist shares in the teaching-preaching charism, we cannot place his ministry of the word in proper perspective without first discussing briefly the importance of all charisms (gifts) in the life of the church. The basis for any charism must be traced back to Jesus himself. His teaching and healing activity as well as his free attitude toward the Old Testament Law and the Temple were seen by his contemporaries and the Evangelists as indications of an extraordinary power. Above all, this power was manifested in his resurrection from the dead. God's saving action in Jesus of Nazareth had replaced the Law as the locus of power and authority, and so life in the Spirit (the power of Christ's presence) became the life-force of the church. One who confesses Jesus as Lord and Christ (1 Cor 12:3) belongs to the body of Christ, the realm of the Holy Spirit in which each member achieves salvation and is empowered to serve others.

Charism, then, is the unfolding of Christ's power in the many members of his body. It is not some unexplained spiritual force, nor is it confined to extraordinary displays. Rather it is directly related to Jesus and permeates the everyday life of the Christian community. Since grace (*charis*) is the new sphere which man enters through God's saving action, the various charisms become the manifestation and individuation of that grace. Thus every structure or office which arises out of the concrete needs of the church can only be seen as auxiliary or secondary to that charismatic structure which is the very foundation of the church.

Charisms do not exist for the individual's glorification but are directed to the service of others. The catechist of our time is charged with understanding and explaining Christian faith—something to which he is already existentially committed. The catechist's service arises from his charism for the building up of the Christian community and must be viewed as a unique instance of that ministry of the word which was exercised in the earliest church by apostles, prophets, teachers and evangelists. We will only understand catechesis in the 20th century if we have grasped the biblical notion of the ministry of the word as first of all and fundamentally a charism flowing from the power of Christ.

Ministers of the Word

Of all the figures responsible for the books of the New Testament the only one about whom we have more than a smattering of autobiographical information is the apostle Paul. Something of a storm-center in the early church, Paul was forced on several occasions to present defenses of his apostleship in reply to attacks from those within and those outside the church. What is especially significant for our theme is that Paul conceived his own ministry as fundamentally a ministry of the word, and so we can glimpse how an individual in the decisive years of the church's spread through the Mediterranean world understood and explained this kind of ministry. While he presents striking apologies for his activity in Gal 1—2 and 2 Cor 10—13, I have chosen to analyze Paul's statement in 1 Thes 2:1-16 because it is his earliest (written in the early 50's of the 1st century) and perhaps most compact reflection on the ministry of the word.

First of all, it is clear that Paul sees himself as an instrument of God's power. He maintains that he has been approved by God to be entrusted with the gospel and that his only aim is to please God (1 Thes 2:4). His relationship is such with his people that he is ready to share with them not only the gospel of God but also his very own self (2:8). He pictures himself as a gentle nurse taking care of her children (2:7) and as a father exhorting his own (2:11). All this is in the service, not of the word of men, but of "what it really is, the word of God, which is at work in you believers (2:13)." This last statement is particularly important, for it shows that for Paul the word of God is an active force having its own power. Paul as an apostle is privileged to be the active bearer of that power.

Paul's labor as a minister of the word is not undertaken for personal gain or comfort. He does not seek glory from men, and he even forgoes the privileges which being an apostle might bring (2:6). In order not to be a burden to anyone when engaged in his preaching activity he worked night and day, presumably at some kind of manual labor, to pay his own way (2:9). His behavior toward other members of the community could only be assessed as "holy and righteous and blameless (2:10)."

Yet this innocent and highly commendable effort aroused considerable opposition. Paul had been accused of preaching error and immorality (2:3) and had been slandered as a flatterer and a greedy person (2:5). More concretely, he had already experienced suffering and shameful treatment at Philippi (2:2; see Acts 16:19-40) and had been expelled from Palestine by his Jewish kinsmen (2:15). In his own sufferings and in those of the church at Thessalonica Paul urges himself and others to recall that Christ Jesus underwent similar treatment (2:15).

The allusion to sharing in the same fate as Jesus did leads us finally to consider what it was that Paul was preaching. He describes it as the "gospel of God" (2:2, 8, 9), the "gospel" (2:4) and as the "word of God" (2:13). Paul's message was the good news about what God had done in the death and resurrection of Jesus of Nazareth. As such, it was the extension of Jesus' own preaching of the kingdom of God, for in Jesus the kingdom was inaugurated.

From this analysis several aspects of the ministry of the word emerge: Paul understands himself as the instrument of divine power. Personal gain or comfort are not even considered significant. Opposition and persecution along with charges stemming from jealousy and ignorance are his lot. Yet he bears with these slights and pains because he is consumed with zeal to preach the gospel of God, the good news about Jesus Christ.

Because it is directed to the Twelve as a group (and, by extension, to all ministers of the word) rather than to an individual, the so-called "mission charge" in Mt 10 may offer us a slightly different approach to the ministry of the word. After the Sermon on the Mount (Mt 5—7) Matthew presents three triads of miracle stories interrupted by sayings on discipleship (Mt 8:1 — 9:34) intended to illustrate the power and authority of Jesus. Although his ministry of teaching, preaching and healing is producing remarkable results, he recognizes the need for disciples to continue his ministry to the "sheep without a shepherd" (Mt 9:35-36).

At the beginning of the speech Jesus is said to have transferred his power and authority to the Twelve (10:1). In other words, those who continue his mission share in his power, for he is acting through them. At the time of Jesus there were many itinerant teachers of Greek philosophies and other wisdoms wandering about the Mediterranean world. With the development of Christianity as a historical force and the rise of Christian missionary activity the real problem for the members of the church was to distinguish between true and false prophets. So the "mission charge" in Mt 10 served both as a handbook for Christian ministers of the word and as a checklist for the people to whom they ministered. In this framework we can now see what dimensions the text offers for our understanding of the ministry of the word.

The Twelve are told to preach that the kingdom of heaven is at hand (10:7)—the same message which was central to the preaching of Jesus himself. They are told to expect to be able to do the wonderful things done first by their Lord through whose power they act. They are not to make the preaching of the gospel a financial proposition; what they received without pay (the gospel), they should give without pay (10:8). They are not to store up money or supplies for their journeys or concern themselves with social climbing and bettering their situation (10:9-13). If the disciple is not heard, then he must move on and consign those who refuse to listen to God's judgment (10:14-15). In spite of their wisdom and innocence the disciples will meet serious opposition from both Jews and Roman officials. When forced to appear in court, they should not be afraid because the Spirit is speaking through them. For the lower and lower-middle-class people who formed the bulk of the first Christian communities the prospect of articulating a public defense of their faith in a court would have been terrifying. Only the conviction that they were instruments of the Spirit sustained them (10:16-20). The disciples also have to expect opposition even from their closest relatives (10:21-22, 34-39) because of their convictions. In fact, they should expect opposition precisely because their Lord and Master received the same treatment (10:24-25). Yet rejection, persecution and opposition cannot stop the spread of the word, and so the disciples should not be afraid (10:26, 28, 31). Their task is to acknowledge Christ before men (10:32-33). The "mission charge" ends with a saying that summarizes the whole and makes explicit the foundation of all Christian ministry: "He who receives you receives me, and he who receives me receives him who sent me (10:40)." Just as the Father had sent Jesus into the world, now Jesus sends the disciples.

Such a careful study of Mt 10 allows us again to list several important characteristics of the minister of the word: He perceives himself as an instrument of God's power. His activity is not undertaken for financial gain or physical comfort. In spite of rejection he is compelled to continue preaching the word. His ministry is an extension of the ministry of Jesus. I consider the correspondences between this text and 1 Thes 2:1-16 to be remarkable proof that we are dealing with a notion familiar and acceptable to most members of the early church.

Content of the Word

We have seen that the Twelve are sent forth to proclaim the word about the kingdom of heaven and that Paul preaches the "gospel of God," and we suggested that both expressions describe the good news about what God has done in Jesus of Nazareth. To explore the content of this "word" in more detail and to explain what it is to which the minister of the word bears witness, we have chosen to examine 1 Cor 15:3b-5 and Acts 2:14-42.

In 1 Cor 15:3b-5 Paul cites what he himself introduces as the gospel which he received and transmitted to the people of Corinth. Writing in the mid-50's of the 1st century, Paul claims that his preaching is not some private fantasy or personal creation: "For I delivered to you as of first importance what I also received . . ." Some have speculated that Paul received this summary of the gospel from Peter at

Jerusalem in A.D. 36 (Gal. 1:18) while others have seen it as a fragment of a Palestinian church hymn. At least, this profession of faith, cited as an already traditional piece, is obviously older than the document in which it appears and does purport to reflect the beliefs of the early Christian community at large. This means that in 1 Cor 15:3b-5 we have a very early and very significant capsule statement of the church's faith. As such, it tells us much about the content both of Paul's preaching and of the common belief of Christians.

According to this confession Jesus is described as the Christ—the Messiah, the Son of David—of Jewish expectation and is said to have "died for our sins in accordance with the Scriptures"; that is, he fulfilled the prophecies of the Old Testament in his life and death (1 Cor 15:3b). He was buried (he was dead and buried; he was really dead), but he was raised from the dead on the third day. By implying that the Father raised up Jesus the confession suggests that he has been exalted. Again, all this was in accordance with the Old Testament Scriptures (15:4). The risen Lord appeared to Peter (called by his Aramaic name "Cephas"—a sign of the confession's origin in the Semitic-speaking community) and then to the Twelve (15:5).

So Paul's ministry of the word was not founded upon a vague sentiment or a good feeling, but on an objective corpus of beliefs. His advice to the communities which he founded flowed from a gospel with real content. In fact, C. H. Dodd had noted long ago that comparison of the traditional formulas cited by Paul (such as 1 Cor 15:3b-5), Paul's own summaries of the gospel and the speeches attributed to the various apostles in Acts reveals a fundamental pattern of early Christian preaching: the Davidic descent of Jesus as guarantee of his Messiahship, his death and resurrection according to the Scriptures, his consequent exaltation to the right hand of God as Lord and Christ, his deliverance of men from sin and into new life, and his return. All these items but the last are present in two-and-one-half verses of 1 Cor 15:3b-5—a remarkably compact statement of the early church's understanding of the content of the word.

We mentioned that the same pattern can be discerned in the speeches given by the apostles in Acts 2:14-42; 3:12-26; 4:24-30; 5:30-42; 10:34-43 and 13:16-41. C. H. Dodd maintained that these discourses represented the preaching of the earliest Palestinian churches, but more recent studies have cast doubt on this assertion. At any rate, what is striking about the passages is that, no matter who the speaker may be, the pattern of the speech is basically the same. When Luke composed Acts between A.D. 80 and 100 (according to the scholarly consensus), his aim in including these discourses was not so much to provide interesting historical information about the past as it was to present examples of his own ideals of missionary preaching. Whatever the origin of the speeches, the fact that Luke offers them as exemplars for his own time is beyond doubt. What is even more extraordinary is that these models for late 1st century ministers of the word correspond very closely in structure, phraseology and tone to what is probably the earliest example of Christian preaching which we have (1 Cor 15:3b-5).

In Acts 2:14-42 we are told that Jesus of Nazareth who was God's agent was delivered up according to the divine foreknowledge and plan and was crucified and killed. But God raised him up (2:22-24). All this was in accordance with Ps 16: "He was not abandoned to Hades, nor did his flesh see corruption (2:31)." In the light of several Old Testament texts it is fair to conclude that "God has made him both Lord and Christ, this Jesus whom you crucified (2:36)." This action of God in Jesus brings about the forgiveness of sins and the gift of the Holy Spirit (2:38). In Christ the new age, the "last days" of Joel 2:28, has already begun. A listing of essential elements in the speech reveals a striking similarity with the confession in 1 Cor 15:3b-5: fulfillment of the Old Testament Scriptures in Jesus' Davidic descent and especially in his death and resurrection, his exaltation to the Father's right hand, deliverance from sin and bestowal of new life, and the inauguration of the new age in Christ.

From these two studies (and their results could be duplicated in many New Testament texts) we are led to conclude that the "word" in the New Testament has a fixed, though somewhat limited, content. Therefore, it is clear that the ministry of the word then and today is not the result of personal whim but, at its root, consists in transmitting and interpreting the basic gospel message. The practice of the four Evangelists illustrates our point beautifully. Their aim was both to remain faithful to the tradition about Jesus (transmission) and also to apply that tradition to the issues facing the church some 40 or 50 years after Jesus' death and resurrection (interpretation). Just as Paul also did, so must every Christian minister of the word bring the gospel to men in his own day and articulate its true significance for human existence in the categories of his time.

The Dynamic Power Behind the Ministry of the Word

Having explored some New Testament perspectives on those who exercise the ministry of the word and on the content of that ministry, we must now examine why people in the early church conceived their activity in terms of the "word" at all. While we could easily and correctly point to the influence of Old Testament prophetic terminology and to the predominance of oral communication in Jesus' time, a more theological and probably more fundamental reason lies in the identification of Jesus with the Word (*logos*) as seen in Jn 1:1-18. Most critics see Jn 1:1-18 as an early Christian hymn to which parenthetical material has been added in vv. 6-8, 13 and 15. Whatever the origin of the *logos* terminology (the Old Testament word of the Lord, personified Wisdom, the Law, the Memra of the Targums, etc.), the point of the identification is that Jesus as the embodiment of divine revelation communicates this revelation to mankind. The equation of Jesus and the *logos* is made explicit only in the Johannine corpus (see also 1 Jn 1:1-4), but the belief it attempts to articulate was shared by other biblical writers.

Jesus' task as the communicator of divine revelation is described in Jn 1:1-18 by sketching the function of the Word in the history of salvation. Attempting to echo the cadences of Gen 1:1 ("In the beginning . . ."), the hymn first depicts the Word as eternal, as accompanying God and as divine (Jn 1:1-2). By stating that all creation was made through the *logos* the text imples that creation itself is a revelation of God. Again, the light-darkness imagery must be a reminiscence of the Old Testament creation narrative in Gen 1. In the act of creation the *logos* communicates his own life (eternal life?) which becomes the light of men. So the opening section of this early church hymn which now introduces the Fourth Gospel tells of the Word whose activity in creation revealed something about who and what God is (Jn 1:1-5).

The next major section (Jn 1:9-12) concerns the Word's role in the world and in Israel before the incarnation. Although many scholars view this section as a description of Jesus' earthly ministry primarily because of the parenthesis about John the Baptist in 1:6-8, to me and to many others the passage makes better sense when understood in the light of the Word's activity in Old Testament times prior to his becoming flesh (1:14). That true light was in the world (*kosmos* in a neutral sense) made through his agency, but was rejected by the world (*kosmos* in a negative sense as antagonistic to God) and even by his own people Israel. Yet those who received the Word became children of God (in Jn only Jesus is the "Son" of God). So in this section of the Prologue the Word is viewed as the inspiring and guiding force expressed in the Old Testament itself by the "word of Lord" and as the figure of Wisdom.

The final tableau (1:14-18) shows how the Word who was in the beginning with God and was himself God (1:1-2) became flesh in human history and dwelt among us men (1:14). His glory is the glory of the only Son from the Father (1:15). The grace and truth which he has brought have been given to us; Jesus is thus greater than Moses who was merely the bearer of the Law (1:16-17). The Word, the only Son who is in complete communication with the Father, has made the Father known (1:18).

According to the Prologue, God has revealed himself. He has spoken through his *logos* in creation, in the period of the Old Testament, and, most emphatically and abundantly, in Jesus Christ. God communicates himself and reveals himself. In our discussion of the charismatic basis of Christian ministry we observed that all ministry flows from the authority of Jesus as the unique revealer of the Father. Our analysis of Jn 1:1-18 shows, in particular, how all ministries of the word flow from the Word himself—Jesus Christ—and that we ministers of the word in the church today share in, and continue on, his ministry. In short, the dynamic power behind all ministry of the word is the Word himself.

Concluding Remarks

At the start of our study on the ministry of the word we defined as our goal the presentation of some New Testament perspectives on this topic. The texts we have chosen for analysis are considered important ones by New Testament specialists and provide, in my opinion, a solid biblical foundation for the general theology of the ministry of the word of which catechesis, according to the directory, is but one manifestation. We cautioned against assuming that one could or should transfer the structures and functions of the earliest church to the church of our time, but we also observed that there is theological wisdom in these texts which spans the ages. We warned against confusing catechesis with preaching, but we also remarked that both ultimately depend upon a common theology.

Catechesis, then, is a unique ministry of the word, an example of a sphere in which the Christian of today can build up the body of Christ (1 Cor 12:27-31; Rom 12:1-8; Eph 4:11-16). The catechist with his zeal to communicate the good news can be an instrument of divine power. At any rate, he takes up the task out of a sincere desire to share with others something he believes in rather than out of a desire for personal gain or comfort (1 Thes 2:1-16; Mt 10). His task is to hand on the gospel (that Jesus who died and was buried and was raised from the dead and, exalted to God's right hand, delivers man from sin and gives new life) in ways which are intelligible to people of his own age (1 Cor 15:3b-5; Acts 2:14-42). He is empowered for the task by his Lord who himself is aptly called the Word and who has made known the Father (Jn 1:1-18).

5. MATTHEAN STUDIES SINCE JOACHIM ROHDE

The publication of Joachim Rohde's *Die redaktionsge-schichtliche Methode*[1] in 1966 marked a significant point in the history of modern Gospel criticism, for its author attempted both to clarify the redaction-critical method and to summarize the major redaction-critical analyses of the Synoptic Gospels published up to that time. According to Rohde, the method proceeds from the realization that the Evangelists' choice of material, the order in which they placed what they had collected, and the alterations they made in the traditional matter, are determined by their theologies. The redaction critic wants to know why the gathering and ordering of the various traditions about Jesus have led to this particular form of a Gospel. He wants to know what these materials meant for the Evangelist and for the community in which he lived and for which he wrote.[2] As a conclusion to his section on Matthew's Gospel, Rohde called attention to the two major problems for which different solutions had been offered—the Jewish Christianity of

[1]The revision of part of his 1962 doctoral dissertation presented to the theological faculty of the Humboldt University in Berlin. It was further revised by the author and translated by D. M. Barton as *Rediscovering the Teaching of the Evangelists* (Philadelphia: Westminster, 1969); our references are to this edition.

[2]*Ibid.*, 1-46.

the Gospel and the separation of Matthew's church from the synagogue. On these two problems, W. Trilling and G. Strecker on the one hand, and G. Bornkamm, G. Barth, and R. Hummel on the other, represented differing points of view. Trilling and Strecker, however, had made it probable for Rohde that the separation of Matthew's church from Judaism had already taken place and that it was therefore no longer possible to speak of Matthew's Jewish Christianity, i.e. Christianity still based in the synagogue. Also discussed were H. J. Held's study of Matthew as interpreter of the miracle stories, M. J. Fiedler's analysis of Matthew's understanding of righteousness, and M. Punge's work on eschatology and salvation history in the Gospel.[3]

Rohde's book was welcomed as a useful compendium, but it was criticized for coming too early in the history of redaction criticism, for not clarifying the objectives and procedures of the method, and for failing to confront the scholarly issues directly.[4] Now, some ten years after the original publication, may be a good time to survey what progress has been made in applying redaction-critical techniques to the study of Matthew's Gospel. We have begun our own survey with works bearing a 1965 publication date and have included whatever pertinent material has come to our attention by early 1975. Commentaries,[5] detailed exegeses of particular passages, and works of popularization have been excluded. We are concerned only with those books and major articles that adopt the redaction-critical method and have as their primary interest Matthew's method of composition, the Christian community in which he lived and for which he wrote, or his theological outlook.

---

³*Ibid.,* 47-112.

⁴See V. Hasler, *TZ* 24 (1968) 56-58; W. G. Thompson, *Bib* 50 (1969) 136-39; and M. D. Goulder, *JTS* 20 (1969) 596-99.

⁵Two recently published commentaries that employ the redaction-critical method are D. Hill's *The Gospel of Matthew* (London: Oliphants, 1972) and E. Schweizer's *Das Evangelium nach Matthäus* (NTD 2; Göttingen: Vandenhoeck & Ruprecht, 1973).

Matthew's Method of Composition

Redaction critics have generally assumed that Matthew used Mark's Gospel, the source Q that he had in common with Luke, and special material (M). Thus, most redaction critics[6] have focused (and quite successfully, we believe) on the distinctive passages in Mt, the ways in which sections begin and end, and the changes in wording and order introduced by the Evangelist into his putative sources. At the Pittsburgh Festival of the Gospels held in 1970, G. Bornkamm[7] tested out the so-called "two-source theory" by examining Mt 18 and concluded that this hypothesis can be sustained. Indeed, the success of redaction criticism in clarifying the theologies of Matthew and Luke was hailed as the most important new argument for Markan priority.[8] On the same occasion, however X. Léon-Dufour[9] questioned whether redaction criticism must be tied to the postulate of the two-source theory and tried to illustrate what benefits might accrue to Matthean studies by beginning with A. Gaboury's[10] theory of multiple sources. W. R. Farmer's revival of the Griesbach hypothesis (Luke used Mt, and Mark used both Mt and Lk) continues to find supporters and critics.[11] A. Fuchs[12] investigated the healings of the two blind men in Mt 9:27-31 and 20:29-34 in relation to their Synoptic parallels and postulated the existence of a second

[6]C. E. Carlston, "Interpreting the Gospel of Matthew," *Interpretation* 29 (1975) 3-12. See also R. H. Stein, "What is Redaktionsgeschichte?" *JBL* 88 (1969) 45-56.

[7]"The Authority to 'Bind' and 'Loose' in the Church in Matthew's Gospel: The Problem of Sources in Matthew's Gospel," *Perspective* 11 (1970) 37-50.

[8]J.M. Robinson, "On the *Gattung* of Mark (and John)," *Perspective* 11 (1970) 101-02.

[9]"*Redaktionsgeschichte* of Matthew and Literary Criticism," *Perspective* 11 (1970) 9-35.

[10]*La structure des évangiles synoptiques. La structure-type à l'origine des Synoptiques* (Suppl. to NovT 22; Leiden: Brill, 1970). See also M.-E. Boismard's work in *Synopse des quatres Evangiles en français,* Tome 2, *Commentaire* (Paris: Cerf, 1972).

[11]R. H. Fuller, E. P. Sanders, and T. R. W. Longstaff, "The Synoptic Problem: After Ten Years," *Perkins Journal* 28 (1975) 63-74.

[12]*Sprachliche Untersuchungen zu Matthäus und Lukas. Ein Beitrag zur Quellenkritik* (AB 49; Rome: Biblical Institute Press, 1971).

edition of Mk on which Mt and Lk depend. H.-T. Wrege[13] analyzed the Sermon on the Mount and argued that Matthew and Luke did not have a common written source on which to draw. According to him, Mt 5—7 and Lk 6:20-49 depend on different oral traditions. We should also draw attention to H. P. West's contention[14] that Matthew used a primitive version of Lk in composing his Gospel and R. T. Simpson's[15] and W. Wilkins's[16] view that Luke used Mt. Finally, M. D. Goulder[17] has argued that Mt is an adaptation and expansion of Mk by midrash and depends on no written source other than Mk and only to a small extent on oral tradition. According to Goulder, Mt was written to be read in Christian worship during the course of the year, as a cycle of readings following the Jewish festal lectionary.

While no one of these challenges to the traditional theory of sources has yet won general scholarly assent, they have at least inspired a growing tendency to look at passages or series of passages as they have been given new and final form by Matthew. W. G. Thompson's[18] study of Mt 17:22—18:35 provides a good example. For him, there are two stages in redaction criticism: (1) vertical, verse-by-verse examination of the text aimed at identifying Matthean vocabulary and style and at isolating the Evangelist's redactional techniques;[19] (2) horizontal comparison with the corresponding material in Mk and Lk to determine where there is literary

[13]*Die Überlieferungsgeschichte der Bergpredigt* (WUNT 9; Tübingen: Mohr-Siebeck, 1968).

[14]"A Primitive Version of Luke in the Composition of Matthew," *NTS* 14 (1967) 75-95.

[15]"The Major Agreements of Matthew and Luke against Mark," *NTS* 12 (1966) 273-84.

[16]"Zur Frage der literarischen Beziehung zwischen Matthäus und Lukas," *NovT* 8 (1966) 48-57.

[17]*Midrash and Lection in Matthew* (London: SPCK, 1974). For a critique, see J. D. M. Derrett, "Midrash in Matthew," *HeyJ* 16 (1975) 51-56.

[18]*Matthew's Advice to a Divided Community. Mt. 17, 22-18, 35* (AB 44; Rome: Biblical Institute Press, 1970).

[19]In an earlier study, "Reflection on the Composition of Mt 8:1—9:34," *CBQ* 33 (1971) 365-88, Thompson used only the first step of his method. For another redaction-critical analysis of Mt 8—9, see C. Burger, "Jesu Taten nach Matthäus 8 und 9," *ZTK* 70 (1973) 272-87.

contact, which is more primitive, and which theory about sources best explains the data. Here the acceptance of the two-source theory comes at the end of an inductive analysis.[20] Thompson now prefers the term "composition criticism"[21] to describe his work; others might call it "inductive structuralism." Whatever the term employed, critics of the future will probably show greater interest in the Gospel as a whole in its final form than they have in the past.

In studies concerning the structure of Mt, B. W. Bacon's "five book" hypothesis[22] has found little support. According to this theory, Matthew arranged his narrative and discourse material into five major sections in order to make a correspondence with the Pentateuch. This procedure has been criticized for overlooking the discourses in Mt 11 and 23, making the infancy and passion narratives into mere appendices to the whole, and failing to point to convincing correspondences in content between the Pentateuch and Matthew's "five books." P. Rolland[23] has tried to rescue the hypothesis by standing it on its head. He sees a parallelism between Mt 1—4 and Pentateuch: 1:1—2:15 (Gen), 2: 16—3:12 (Exod), 3:13-17 (Lev), 4:1-7 (Num), and 4:8-16 (Deut). Then the five major discourses are seen to be arranged in the inverse order of the Pentateuch and in chiastic symmetry with the prologue.

H. B. Green[24] prefers to begin with Matthew's adherence to Mark's order from Mt 11 onward. He has worked out a parabolic structure that rises to an apex in ch. 11 and falls away again. On the two sides of the parabola one can discern correspondences between chs. 10 and 12—13 (mis-

[20]See also D. Senior, "The Passion Narrative in the Gospel of Matthew," in *L'Évangile selon Matthieu. Rédaction et théologie* (ed. M. Didier; BETL 29; Gembloux: Duculot, 1972) 343-57.

[21]"An Historical Perspective in the Gospel of Matthew," *JBL* 93 (1974) 244.

[22]"The 'Five Books' of Matthew Against the Jews," *The Expositor* 15/8 (1918) 56-66; *Studies in Matthew* (New York: Henry Holt, 1930).

[23]"From the Genesis to the End of the World: the Plan of Matthew's Gospel," *BTB* 2 (1972) 155-76.

[24]"The Structure of St. Matthew's Gospel," in *Studia Evangelica* (TU 102; Berlin: Akademie, 1968) 47-59.

sion, mission rejected), 8—9 and 14—18 (miracles per-
formed, miracles rejected), 5—7 and 19—23 (teaching
presented, teaching rejected), 3—4 and 24—25 (Christ's
manifestation to Israel, his warning about the coming judgment), and 1—2 and 26—28 (the new-born Christ, his death
and resurrection). Thus Matthew has taken the falling side
of the parabola from Mk and balanced it off with a rising
side.

J. D. Kingsbury[25] wishes to subsume the "fivefold formula" ("and when Jesus finished . . .") found at the end of
each major discourse under the formula "from that time
Jesus began . . ." in Mt 4:17 and 16:21. This latter formula is
seen as indicating the broadest divisions of the gospel: the
person of Jesus Messiah (1:1—4:16), the proclamation of
Jesus Messiah (4:17—16:20), and the suffering, death and
resurrection of Jesus Messiah (16:21—28:20). The fact that
the last two sections each contain three principal summaries
(4:23-25; 9:35; 11:1; and 16:21; 17:22-23; 20:17-19) is seen as
further proof of the internal unity of both. L. Ramaroson[26]
has discerned in Mt a plan aimed at describing the mystery
of the death that gives life, while K. Meschke[27] has suggested
that Peter's confession in 16:13-20 functions as the midpoint
dividing the gospel into two almost equal parts. While all of
these scholars find Bacon's hypothesis inadequate, there is a
startling lack of agreement as to what the overall structure
really is. But at least there is a recognition that in determin-
ing the structure of the Gospel the several structural factors
(content, use of Mk, formulas, etc.) must be taken into
account.

Matthew's Community

Monographs on parts of the Gospel have shed light on
some of the problems confronting Matthew's community. A

[25]"The Structure of Matthew's Gospel and His Concept of Salvation-History,"
CBQ 35 (1973) 451-74.
[26]"La structure du premier Évangile," *Science et Esprit* 26 (1974) 69-112.
[27]"Matteusevangeliets mitt," *Svensk Teologisk Kvartalskrift* 48 (1972) 119-21.

detailed analysis of Mt 13:1-52 has led J. D. Kingsbury[28] to list these issues: materialism, secularism, spiritual slothfulness, hatred among Christians, lovelessness, apostasy, and lawlessness. From his study of Mt 17:22—18:35, W. G. Thompson[29] concluded that Matthew's community was badly divided. Scandal was a concrete threat (18:5-9), and the need for fraternal correction was urgent (18:15-20). On the positive side, E. Schweizer[30] has described the church of the first Gospel as the body of "these little ones" who are ready to follow Jesus, to remain obedient to the law of God interpreted by Jesus' deeds and words, to reinterpret his instructions ever anew in answer to practical problems, to proclaim his word and let it speak to present situations, and to revive his miraculous power in healings.

Schweizer[31] has found what he believes to be confirmation for the localization of Matthew's church in Syria in the *Apocalypse of Peter* from Nag Hammadi. This treatise offers direct evidence of an ascetic Judaeo-Christian group of "these little ones" with no bishops or deacons, still experiencing heavenly visions and prophetic auditions. E. L. Abel[32] distinguishes between a Jewish-Christian editor who constructed his document between A.D. 64 and 70 and a Gentile editor who produced the final edition of the Gospel at Antioch between A.D. 80 and 105. Most scholars continue to place Mt in Syria or Palestine, but S. van Tilborg[33] maintains that Matthew lived in a world where Judaism was no longer a serious competitor, that he was not a Jew, and that he was possibly the spokesman for the Gentile Christian community of Alexandria. According to

---

[28] *The Parables of Jesus in Matthew 13. A Study in Redaction-Criticism* (Richmond, VA: John Knox, 1969) 135.

[29] *Matthew's Advice,* 266. For other redaction-critical studies of Mt 18, see W. Pesch, *Matthäus als Seelsorger* (Stuttgart: Katholisches Bibelwerk, 1966), and E. Schweizer, "Matthew's View of the Church in his 18th Chapter," *Australian Biblical Review* 21 (1973) 7-14.

[30] "Observance of the Law and Charismatic Activity in Matthew," *NTS* 16 (1970) 213-30.

[31] "The 'Matthean' Church," *NTS* 20 (1974) 216; see also *ZNW* 65 (1974) 139.

[32] "Who Wrote Matthew?" *NTS* 17 (1971) 138-52.

[33] *The Jewish Leaders in Matthew* (Leiden: Brill, 1972).

R. E. Osborne,[34] the parallels between the M material and
Zoroastrian, Mithraic, and Buddhist teachings point to a
final composition of the Gospel in Edessa.

A more fundamental concern than localization is Matthew's relationship to Judaism. W. D. Davies,[35] in the popular version of his massive *Setting of the Sermon on the
Mount* (1964), suggests that Matthew was conscious of
Jamnia as was Jamnia of the new faith and that the shadow
of Jamnia lies over his Gospel. The Sermon on the Mount is
seen by Davies as the deliberate formulation of the Christian moral ideal and tradition at a time when the Mishnah
was coming to birth in Judaism. K. Tagawa[36] has called
attention to the dilemma of the Jewish Christians and said
that for Matthew there can be no Gentile church, for the
Gentile mission is only intended to introduce Gentiles into
the Israel-Christian community. D. R. A. Hare[37] has gone in
a very different (and, we believe, more correct) direction.
The mission to the synagogues and the attendant persecution of missionaries belong to the Evangelist's past. The
failure and abandonment of the mission to Israel result not
in a retreat into apocalypticism but in a redefining of energy
into the Gentile mission. The invitation that Israel refused
so rudely is now to be offered exclusively to the Gentiles
(28:19). S. Légasse[38] has described Matthew's so-called
"anti-Judaism": The Jewish opponents have conducted
themselves hypocritically, have perverted their function as
guides of the people, and have rejected Jesus' teaching and
put him to death. When assessing Matthew's stance toward
the Jews, we must bear in mind that his polemics are
designed to warn Christians against hypocrisy on their own
part, that the heat in these polemics may be due to Jewish

[34]"The provenance of Matthew's gospel," *Studies in Religion/ Sciences Religieuses* 3 (1973) 220-35.

[35]*The Sermon on the Mount* (Cambridge: Cambridge University Press, 1966).

[36]"People and Community in the Gospel of Matthew," *NTS* 16 (1970) 149-62.

[37]*The Theme of Jewish Persecution of Christians in the Gospel According to St.
Matthew* (SNTSMS 6; London: Cambridge University Press, 1967).

[38]L'"anti-judaisme' dans l'Évangile selon Matthieu," in *L'Évangile selon Matthieu,* 417-28.

efforts against the Christian community and/or the convert's zeal to define himself over against what he has rejected, that no hostile actions are urged (on the contrary, see 5:12, 44-47), and that individual Jews are accepted into the church (see 11:28-30).

Another fertile area of Matthean studies has been the groups that appear in the course of the Gospel. U. Luz[39] maintains that the disciples in Mt hear and understand Jesus' teaching and so provide a model or type for the Christian. In the miracle stories the disciples manifest "little faith" (a middle ground between faith and unbelief) and share in the power of the Lord. By avoiding the term "apostle" and by equating the disciple with "brother" and "little one," Matthew fosters the identification of the disciples with members of his own community. Throughout the Gospel, but especially in Mt 28:16-20, he tries to combine two perspectives: The disciple shares in the power of the risen Lord and faithfully transmits the teaching of the earthly Jesus. Along the same lines, M. Sheridan[40] has said that the Twelve are exemplary for all Christians in that, with Jesus' help, they overcome their lack of trust in his power and the Father's care. In addition, they can be seen to represent the leaders of the church, who must always remain the Lord's disciples. E. Cothenet[41] suggests that, according to Matthew, Christian prophets exercise an itinerant ministry (10:41) and perform healings and exorcisms (7:22). Matthew is not opposed to prophecy as such, but feels that it must be judged in accord with the example of the Twelve (Mt 10), the fulfillment of the law brought about in Christ, and the words and deeds of Jesus himself. Schweizer's contention that itinerant prophecy is the only type of ministry admitted by Matthew is dismissed as a manifest exaggeration. The collocation of *prophētēs* and *dikaios* in Mt 10:41;

---

[39]"Die Jünger im Matthäusevangelium," *ZNW* 62 (1971) 141-71.

[40]"Disciples and Discipleship in Matthew and Luke," *BTB* 3 (1973) 235-55.

[41]"Les prophètes chrétiens dans l'Évangile selon saint Matthieu," in *L'Évangile selon Matthieu,* 281-308.

13:17; and 23:29 indicates to D. Hill[42] that *dikaioi* serves as a quasi-technical term and refers to people who have a witnessing or teaching function in the community. P. S. Minear[43] proposes that, far from being an amorphous and neutral category, the crowds (*ochloi*) in Mt play a highly positive role as followers of Jesus. They constitute a major objective of Jesus' ministry in all its aspects. Whether they will remain under the Pharisees or shift over to Jesus and his disciples depends primarily on the faithfulness of the disciples to their commission as teachers. In his study on the Jewish leaders, S. van Tilborg[44] argues that Matthew does not wish to create distinctions among the Jewish groups. He prefers combination formulas ("the Pharisees and Sadducees," "the scribes and Pharisees," and "the chief priests and elders") and looks upon the representatives of Israel as a homogeneous group. These leaders are called "hypocrites," "evildoers," and "murderers"; their guilt is especially stressed in the passion narrative.

There seems to be a somewhat critical attitude toward church leaders at work in the Gospel. While W. Trilling[45] is very cautious about defining the structure of the community, he does suggest that Matthew opposed any Christian personality cult that would reject equality in brotherhood and discipleship and that would view church offices as something other than service (see 23:8-12). P. S. Minear[46] says that Matthew thought of Jesus' disciples as prophets and that the relation between the congregations and the Christian prophets in his own day was roughly analogous to that between the crowds and the disciples in Jesus' day. Matthew thought that Christian leaders faced a double danger: They might become either false prophets or hypo-

---

[42] "*Dikaioi* as a Quasi-Technical Term," *NTS* 11 (1965) 296-302.

[43] "The Disciples and the Crowds in the Gospel of Matthew," ATR, suppl. ser. 3 (1974) 28-44.

[44] *The Jewish Leaders in Matthew.*

[45] "Amt und Amtsverständnis bei Matthäus," *Mélanges Bibliques en hommage au R.P. Beda Rigaux* (Gembloux: Duculot, 1970) 29-44.

[46] "False Prophecy and Hypocrisy in the Gospel of Matthew," *Neues Testament und Kirche. Für Rudolf Schnackenburg* (Freiburg: Herder, 1974) 76-93.

crites. Minear concludes that "Matthew was not so much anti-Jewish as anti-scribe, and not so much anti-scribe as anti-hypocrite, and more concerned with the hypocrisies of church leaders than with those of synagogue leaders." According to H. Frankemölle,[47] Matthew has depicted Peter as the prototype of the church leader: He is pre-eminent but remains subject to temptation and danger. Matthew's critical attitude toward Peter and church leaders is only one element in his broader critical understanding of Christian existence and the church. More recently, Frankemölle[48] has published the most comprehensive study of Matthew's ecclesiology to date in which he discusses "with us" (*meth' hymōn*) as the christological and theological basis of the community, the individual-personal concepts (disciple, son, brother, servant), the collective-metaphorical concepts (*laos, ekklēsia, ethnos*), the promise and protection of salvation, and the Gospel as an interpretation of history. R. Thysman[49] has tried to determine the impact of Matthew's understanding of the church on Christian conduct. He calls attention to Matthew's pastoral presentation of Jesus' demands on the community and the directives for the conduct of those who are "pastors."

Lastly, there is the matter of the relation between the church and the kingdom. W. O. Walker[50] has argued against assuming any distinction between the kingdom of the Son of Man (identified with the Christian church in the present age) and the kingdom of the Father. According to A. Kretzer,[51] the kingdom of heaven manifests itself as a reality governing all that is, coming from heaven to earth, and

[47] "Amtskritik im Matthäus-Evangelium?" *Bib* 54 (1973) 247-62.

[48] *Jahwebund und Kirche Christi. Studien zur Form- und Traditionsgeschichte des "Evangeliums" nach Matthäus* (NTAbh 10; Münster: Aschendorff, 1974). See also J.P. Martin, "The Church in Matthew," *Interpretation* 29 (1975) 41-56.

[49] *Communauté et directives éthiques. La catéchèse de Matthieu* (Gembloux: Duculot, 1974).

[50] "The Kingdom of the Son of Man and the Kingdom of the Father in Matthew. An Exercise in *Redaktionsgeschichte,*" *CBQ* 30 (1968) 573-79.

[51] *Die Herrschaft der Himmel und die Söhne des Reiches. Eine redaktionsgeschichtliche Untersuchung zum Basileiabegriff und Basileiaverständnis im Matthäusevangelium* (Stuttgart: Katholisches Bibelwerk, 1971).

effecting the salvation of mankind. The kingdom has temporal, spatial, and personal-ethical dimensions. First present in Israel and subsequently in Matthew's Christian community, the kingdom will finally extend to all the world. Matthew's community must now produce fruit in doing good.

Matthew's Theology

In attempting to state Matthew's division of history, G. Strecker[52] has placed the "time of Jesus" at the center. This unique, holy, and ideal time in which Jesus was sent to Israel was preceded by the "time of preparation" (the time of the fathers and the prophets) and is followed by the "time of the church" (the time of the world mission lasting until the eschaton). R. Walker[53] has worked out a more elaborate scheme that begins with Abraham and ends with the eschaton. Between these poles there are three major periods: the pre-history of the Messiah, the calling of Israel to the kingdom of heaven, and the calling of the Gentiles. Matthew lives and writes in the third period. J. D. Kingsbury[54] sees only two major epochs: the time of Israel and the time of Jesus. The former was inaugurated by Abraham and the latter by the public ministry of John the Baptist. The two are related as promise and fulfillment. From his analysis of Mt 24:4-14, W. G. Thompson[55] has identified this historical perspective: the past mission to Israel prior to A.D. 70 (vv. 7-8), the present time of external opposition and internal dissension (vv. 9-13), and the end of the age when the mission to all the nations is completed (v. 14). This same historical time-line influenced Matthew as he composed 24:36—25:46; 28:16-20; and 17:22—18:35. Finally J. P.

[52]"Das Geschichtsverständnis des Matthäus," *EvT* 26 (1966) 57-74; see also *JAAR* 35 (1967) 219-30.

[53]*Die Heilsgeschichte im ersten Evangelium* (FRLANT 91; Göttingen: Vandenhoeck & Ruprecht, 1967).

[54]*CBQ* 35 (1973) 451-74.

[55]*JBL* 93 (1974) 243-62.

Meier[56] calls attention to the significance of Jesus' death and resurrection as the eschatological event in which the kingdom breaks into this age in a new way. This explains why the limitations of territory, nation, and Mosaic Law are observed during Jesus' public ministry and why these restrictions fall away after the enthronement of the Son of Man.

Nearly every study of a particular passage or of the Gospel as a whole makes a contribution to the understanding of Matthew's Christology, but the closest thing to a comprehensive statement from a redaction-critical perspective is the series of articles published by J. D. Kingsbury.[57] The term "Son of Man" is the christological title with which Jesus encounters the world, Jews first and then Gentiles, and particularly his opponents and unbelievers. The title "Son of God" extends to every phase of Jesus' life, is the natural complement to the thoroughly Matthean "my Father," and represents the most exalted confession of Matthew's community. *Kyrios* is an auxiliary christological title, the purpose of which is to attribute divine authority to Jesus, as the Christ, Son of David, Son of God, or Son of Man. It is not one of the chief titles with which Matthew develops his Christology. For B. Gerhardsson,[58] Matthew's Jesus is the Son of God who takes it upon himself to be the

[56]"Salvation-History in Matthew: In Search of a Starting Point," *CBQ* 37 (1975) 203-15.

[57]"The Title 'Son of Man' in Matthew's Gospel," *CBQ* 37 (1975) 193-202; "The Title 'Son of God' in Matthew's Gospel," *BTB* 5 (1975) 3-31; "The Title 'Kyrios' in Matthew's Gospel," *JBL* 94 (1975) 246-55; "Form and Message of Matthew," *Interpretation* 29 (1975) 13-24; "Matthew's Redefinition of the Gospel," *Dialog* 12 (1973) 32-37. Several detailed studies of Mt 28:16-20 are significant for understanding Matthew's Christology: Kingsbury, "The Composition and Christology of Matt 28:16-20," *JBL* 93 (1974) 573-84; J. Lange, *Das Erscheinen des Auferstandenen im Evangelium nach Matthäus. Eine traditions- und redaktionsgeschichtliche Untersuchung zu Mt 28, 16-20* (Forschung zur Bibel 11; Würzburg: Echter, 1973); B.J. Hubbard, *The Matthean Redaction of a Primitive Apostolic Commissioning: An Exegesis of Matthew 28:16-20* (SBLDS 19; Missoula, MT: Scholars, 1974).

[58]"Sacrificial Service and Atonement in the Gospel of Matthew," in *Reconciliation and Hope. New Testament Essays on Atonement and Eschatology presented to L. L. Morris on his 60th Birthday* (Grand Rapids: Eerdmans, 1974) 25-35. See

perfect Servant of God in all things. His ministry is a spiritual service of sacrifice and is the perfect prototype for all the children of God who want to be servants of God. His followers are to constitute a place of expiation, a sanctuary of atonement in Israel and for all people. In death Jesus exemplifies perfectly the just man abandoned by God; in his resurrection he is once again given "all power," thus enabling his disciples to take the yoke of his teaching upon them and enter into the vocation of the Servant of God. J. M. Gibbs[59] rejects the description of Jesus as the "new Moses" and points to the notion of Jesus the Son of God as the Torah incarnate: Since the Father's covenanted will is the Torah, so Jesus is the Torah incarnate, the enfleshing of both the demand and the promise of the covenant, for he is "God with us." Along the same lines, M. J. Suggs[60] has suggested that Matthew took over Wisdom speculation from Q but used Wisdom themes in a unique way to identify Jesus with Wisdom—not Wisdom's child but Wisdom incarnate. As the incarnation of Wisdom, Jesus also becomes the embodiment of the Torah. E. P. Blair[61] has characterized Matthew's Jesus as a revealer with unique supernatural knowledge. A. Suhl[62] maintains that Matthew uses "Son of David" to reflect not only acceptance by believers and misunderstanding by the crowds but also spiritual blindness on the part of the leaders of the people. L. Gaston[63] shows how Jesus' messiahship and his rejection by Israel are related: Because Israel has rejected its Messiah, God has rejected Israel. Whether Christians today can accept Matthew's theology of *Unheilsgeschichte* in respect to Israel emerges as

---

also "Utlämnad och övergiven. Till förståelsen av passionshistorien i Matteusevangeliet," *Svensk Exegetisk Årsbok* 32 (1967) 92-120; "Gottes Sohn als Diener Gottes: Messias, Agape und Himmelsherrschaft nach dem Matthäusevangelium," *Studia Theologica* 27 (1973) 73-106.

[59]"The Son of God as the Torah Incarnate in Matthew," *Studia Evangelica* (TU 102; Berlin: Akademie, 1968) 38-46.

[60]*Wisdom, Christology, and Law in Matthew's Gospel* (Cambridge, MA: Harvard, 1970). For a critique, see M.D. Johnson, "Reflections on a Wisdom Approach to Matthew's Christology," *CBQ* 36 (1974) 44-64.

[61]"Jesus and Salvation in the Gospel of Matthew," *McCormick Quarterly* 20 (1967) 301-08.

[62]"Der Davidssohn in Matthäusevangelium," *ZNW* 59 (1968) 57-81.

[63]"The Messiah of Israel As Teacher of the Gentiles," *Interpretation* 29 (1975) 24-40.

an important hermeneutical issue.

In his study of Matthew's use of the OT, R. H. Gundry[64] has examined both the explicit fulfillment quotations and the allusions. According to him, Matthew was his own targumist and drew upon a knowledge of the Hebrew, Aramaic, and Greek textual traditions. Matthew the apostle was a notetaker during the earthly ministry of Jesus, and his notes provided the basis for the bulk of the apostolic Gospel tradition. Such an explanation for the genesis of the quotations and allusions places Gundry outside the mainstream of Matthean scholarship. In R. S. McConnell's[65] view, just as Matthew explains that Jesus fulfils the OT Law by his teaching, even so by means of the fulfillment quotations he shows that Jesus' life and ministry fulfill OT prophecy. In almost every case the OT texts are molded to fit the accomplished life of Christ and not the reverse. The *Sitz im Leben* of the formula quotations is probably missionary preaching, though some school activity may be present. W. Rothfuchs[66] maintains that the fulfillment quotations are to be viewed primarily as an aspect of Matthew's redactional activity. Seeking neither to "prove" Jesus nor to make an apology for his shameful death, Matthew uses the texts to preach Jesus as the Messiah. Thus they are to be located in the early Christian homiletical tradition rather than in a school. L. Hartman[67] has stated three reasons why Matthew cites the OT: to undergird his opinion with another opinion, to make his text more elegant or striking, and to call forth a cluster of associations in his readers' minds. F. Van Segbroeck[68] has summarized the present state of research on Mat-

---

[64] *The Use of the Old Testament in St. Matthew's Gospel with Special Reference to the Messianic Hope* (Suppl. to NovT 18; Leiden: Brill, 1967).

[65] *Law and Prophecy in Matthew's Gospel. The Authority and Use of the Old Testament in the Gospel of St. Matthew* (Theologische Dissertationen 2; Basel: F. Reinhardt, 1969).

[66] *Die Erfüllungszitate des Matthäus-Evangeliums. Eine biblische-theologische Untersuchung* (BWANT 8; Stuttgart-Mainz: Kohlhammer, 1969).

[67] " 'Såsom der ar skrivet'. Några reflexioner over citat som kommunikationsmedel i Matteusevangeliet," *Svensk Exegetisk Årsbok* 35 (1970) 33-43; see also his "Scriptural Exegesis in the Gospel of Matthew and the Problem of Communication," in *L'Évangile selon Matthieu*, 131-52.

[68] "Les citations d'accomplissement dans l'Evangile selon saint Matthieu d'après trois ouvrages récents," in *L'Évangile selon Matthieu*, 107-30.

thew's use of the OT in this way: The formula quotations having a mixed textual form constitute a separate category; the postulate of a collection of OT *testimonia* does not explain the situation; K. Stendahl's thesis[69] that the formula quotations reflect Christian scribal activity similar to that which produced the Qumran pesharim has not won acceptance; the citations reflect the Evangelist's theology and are part of his work as a redactor.

Perhaps the most controversial aspect of Matthean theology involves the Evangelist's attitude toward the OT Law. R. G. Hamerton-Kelly[70] has detected three distinct attitudes toward the Law in Mt: a legally rigorous attitude stressing the details of the Mosaic Law, the view that the Law was abrogated by Jesus to permit the Gentile mission, and Matthew's own understanding that the authority of the traditional halakah had been replaced by the risen Christ as halakist. To H. Simonsen,[71] though Matthew remains more attached than Mark to the Jewish milieu, his thought is not judaizing. The prescriptions of the Law are put aside if they hinder communion with Jesus; obedience to Jesus' message of salvation is incumbent upon all. Along the same lines, R. Banks[72] suggests that the "commandments" of 5:19 refer to Christ's own instructions rather than the Mosaic legislation. He also observes that the major issue for Matthew is how the Law stands with Jesus, not how Jesus stands with the Law. In what is the most extensive redaction-critical treatment of the whole topic to date, A. Sand[73] argues that Matthew is primarily interested in the general thrust of the Mosaic Torah and measures the observance of the Law by one's attitude toward the neighbor and God. In an earlier

[69] *The School of St. Matthew and its Use of the Old Testament* (2nd ed.; Philadelphia: Fortress, 1968).

[70] "Attitudes to the Law in Matthew's Gospel: A Discussion of Matthew 5:18," *Biblical Research* 17 (1972) 19-32.

[71] "Synet på loven i Matteusevangeliet," *Dansk Teologisk Tidsskrift* 36 (1973) 174-94.

[72] "Matthew's Understanding of the Law: Authenticity and Interpretation in Matthew 5:17-20," *JBL* 93 (1974) 226-42.

[73] *Das Gesetz und die Propheten. Untersuchungen zur Theologie des Evangeliums nach Matthäus* (Biblische Untersuchungen 11; Regensburg: Pustet, 1974).

article,[74] Sand pointed to the different meanings of *anomia* in Matthew and Paul: Matthew depends on the OT and regards lawlessness as an offence against the divinely ordained Law; Paul sees lawlessness as an enslaving consequence of the powers of sin, Law, and death.

Conclusion

Having taken up where Rohde left off and having reviewed a decade's research on Matthew's method of composition, community, and theology, we can now list what we perceive to be the major trends of redaction-critical study of the first Gospel during this period: general acceptance of the two-source theory, but greater caution toward assuming it as the only sure basis of study; recognition that Bacon's "five book" hypothesis is inadequate and that the several structural principles in the Gospel have to be taken into account; increased awareness of the severe problems that Matthew had to confront within his community; growing consensus that he writes after the split between church and synagogue; sensitivity to the ways in which he uses the various groups (disciples, prophets, righteous ones, crowds, Jewish leaders) for his own literary and theological purposes; consciousness of Matthew's somewhat critical attitude toward church leaders; perception that he sees a break between the time of the mission to Israel (Mt 10) and the mission to the Gentiles (28:16-20); feeling that a comprehensive description of Matthean Christology from a redaction-critical standpoint is needed; willingness to see the OT formula quotations as part of the Evangelist's redactional activity; and a sense of the complexity of Matthew's attitude toward the Mosaic Law.

---

[74] "Die Polemik gegen 'Gesetzlosigkeit' im Evangelium nach Matthäus und bei Paulus. Ein Beitrag zur neutestamentlichen Überlieferungsgeschichte,"*BZ* 14 (1970) 112-25.

6. "MAKE DISCIPLES OF ALL THE GENTILES" (MT 28:19)

All of us are aware of the importance of the risen Lord's commission to the disciples in Mt 28:16-20 for understanding Matthew's general aims. Furthermore, we all are cognizant of the significance of the phrase *mathēteusate panta ta ethnē* in Matthew's theological outlook, but we also recognize that the phrase is not transparently clear. Does the expression *panta ta ethnē* include the nation of Israel, or is there a deliberate contrast between Israel and the other peoples of the world? In his scheme of salvation history does Matthew consider Israel as belonging to the present or to the past? Did he write his Gospel before or after the definitive split between the church and Judaism?

One simple and concrete way to gain insight into these matters is through a word study of *ethnos/ethnē*. Our paper has five major sections: the use of the term in Judaism and the NT, its appearances in Mt, the case for *panta ta ethnē* as including Israel in Mt, "Jews" and "Gentiles" in Matthean theology, and some patristic interpretations of Mt 28:19. The view presented in this paper is that *mathēteusate panta ta ethnē* means "make disciples of all the Gentiles" and that *panta ta ethnē* does not include the nation of Israel.[1] Our position is that for Matthew the *ethnē* and Israel are two distinct entities in salvation history. Individuals of Jewish heritage (such as Matthew himself) will be accepted into the church, but in Matthew's overall view of salvation history the kingdom of God has been taken away from Israel and given to a nation (*ethnos*) producing the fruits of it (Mt 21:43), i.e., the church. As an entity in salvation history or as a "religious institution" Israel has been replaced by the church.[2]

1. The Use of gôyîm and ethnē in Judaism and the NT

Our treatment of *gôyîm* and *ethnē* in Judaism and the NT must necessarily be brief and somewhat sketchy; our paper is not intended as an exhaustive study of these terms. It is enough to indicate that when Matthew's church was taking shape *gôyîm* and *ethnē* referred to that collective of nations other than Israel and also to those individuals who were not Jews.[3] In the period of the monarchy *gôyîm* had denoted above all the encircling foreign nations that were in competition with the nation of Israel, but in the Persian and Hellenistic periods these nations were submerged under an imperial administration not greatly concerned about old

[1] The earliest critical presentation of the case for "Gentiles" in Mt 28:19 of which we are aware is that of B. Weiss, *Das Matthäus-Evangelium* (8th ed., Göttingen: Vandenhoeck & Ruprecht, 1890) 497-98. Better known in the English-speaking world is the article by K. W. Clark, "The Gentile Bias in Matthew," *JBL* 66 (1947) 165-72. For more recent treatments see D. R. A. Hare, *The Theme of Jewish Persecution of Christians in the Gospel According to St. Matthew (SNTSMS 6;* New York—London: Cambridge University Press, 1967) 148 and R. Walker, *Die Heilsgeschichte im ersten Evangelium (FRLANT* 91; Göttingen: Vandenhoeck & Ruprecht, 1967) 111-13 and the literature cited there.

[2] See H. Frankemölle, "Amtskritik im Matthäus-Evangelium?" *Bib* 54 (1973) 247-62 and *Jahwebund und Kirche Christi. Studien zur Form-und Traditionsgeschichte des "Evangeliums" nach Matthäus* (NTAbh 2/10; Münster: Aschendorff, 1974).

[3] See G. Bertram and K. L. Schmidt, *"ethnos, ethnikos,"* in TDNT 2 (1964) 364-72.

national boundaries. Then *gôyîm* came more and more to represent not national groups such as the Egyptians or the Greeks but rather one overarching collective—non-Jewish mankind. The term *gôyîm* was also used to describe all the individuals who did not belong to the chosen people. Assimilation to the *gôyîm* was perceived as a constant threat to traditional religion and culture.

This new usage is clearly witnessed in the Qumran writings. The *Zadokite Document* enjoins: "No man shall rest in a place near to the *gôyîm* on the day of the Sabbath" (CD 11:14-15). This statement makes more sense if *gôyîm* refers to Gentile settlements in Palestine (or elsewhere) rather than to specific national groups such as the Egyptians or Greeks. Similarly CD 12:8-9 states: "No man shall sell an animal or bird that is clean to the *gôyîm,* in order that they sacrifice them not." The prohibition here concerns sale to individual Gentiles, not to national groups. In the *War Scroll* there are several references to *gwy hbl.* Y. Yadin[4] apparently takes *gwy* as a defective spelling for the construct plural and, because of the prefixed *kwl,* translates *gwy hbl* in 1QM 4:12 and 6:6 as "all nations of vanity." In 1QM 9:8-9 ("they shall not desecrate the oil of their priestly anointment with the blood of *gwy hbl*") again the translation "nation(s) of vanity" is preferred by all commentators, but it is tempting to take *gwy* as a singular ("the blood of a vain Gentile").[5] Then we would have a reference to the Mishnaic usage whereby *gôy* refers to an individual non-Jew (*Demai* 6:10; *Betzah* 3:2) and *yiśra'el* refers to an individual Jew (*Yebamoth* 16:5). At any rate, these (and many other) Hebrew texts show that *gôyîm* refers to the whole collection of non-Jews rather than to specific national groups, and they hint at a usage that would describe individual non-Jews also as *gôyîm.*

In the Septuagint *ethnē* established itself as the usual

---

[4]Y. Yadin *The Scroll of the War of the Sons of Light Against the Sons of Darkness* (tr. B. and C. Rabin; New York—London: Oxford, 1962) *ad loc.*

[5]But *gwy hbl* is used in 1QM 11:9 preceded by *šb 't* ("seven"). It should be noted that the *plene* spelling *gwyy* is found in 1QM 14:7. The singular *gwy* may be intentional in 1QM 15:2.

rendering for *gôyîm* and meant "nations," usually "foreign nations." The Greek singular *laos* was preferred for Hebrew *'am* and was used primarily for Israel. But in the LXX for Ezra 9:11 (Esdras Beta 9:11) the translator employs *laoi tōn ethnōn* to translate the Hebrew *'ammê hā 'ărāṣôt*. In such a rendering *ethnōn* would be redundant unless it meant "non-Jewish mankind," i.e. Gentiles. In 1 Maccabees, which is usually regarded as a translation from a Hebrew original, the use of *gôyîm* to refer to non-Jews is reflected in those passages where *ethnē* is found. For example, at 5:9 *ta ethnē ta en tē Galaad* must refer to "Gentiles." Similarly in 5:38 *panta ta ethnē ta kyklō ēmōn* must mean "all the Gentiles around us." Other examples of *ethnos/ethnē* to describe Gentiles in intertestamental literature can be found in section 3 of this article.

This same use of *ethnē* as a designation for non-Jews is well attested in the NT, and for this reason it is frequently rendered by "Gentiles" (e.g., at Rom 11:11-13; Gal 2:12). In some passages it has the additional meaning of idolators or pagans (1 Cor 12:21; 1 Pet 2:12; 4:3). One difficulty with the Greek term *ethnos* was that it could not be used in the singular to describe an individual Gentile. Thus Luke and Paul find it necessary to use *hellēn* ("Greek") when referring to an individual Gentile (Acts 16:1; Rom 1:16; 10:12; Gal 2:3; 3:28; Col 3:11; see also Mark's use of the feminine *hellēnis* in 7:26 to indicate the Syrophoenician woman's *religious* background). Perhaps the adjective *ethnikos* (Mt 5:47; 6:7; 18:17; 3 Jn 7) as a designation for an individual Gentile was considered as pejorative by Greek-speaking Jews. It is certainly employed as such in Mt 18:17, the only instance of the singular in the NT. One wonders whether we may be dealing here with an underlying *gôy*. John avoids even the plural *ethnē*, preferring *hellēnes* (7:35; 12:20), while using *ethnos*, never *laos*, as a designation for Israel (11:48, 50, 52; 18:35).[6]

---

[6]The use of *ethnos* for Israel, found only in Lk-Acts and Jn in the NT, is particularly noticeable in Tobit, 4 Maccabees, Philo, and Josephus.

The purpose of this survey has been to suggest that in
Matthew's time *gôyîm* and *ethnē* would not have referred to
those specific national groups (Egyptians, Greeks, etc.) that
impinged upon the nation of Israel. Rather, these terms
would convey the notion of that whole collective of nations
(the Gentile nations) other than Israel as well as those
individual non-Jews (the Gentiles) who made up that
collective.

2. *The Appearances of* ethnos/ethnē *in Matthew*

In three places we have *ethnos/ethnē* in phrases that
Matthew shares with Mark and Luke. Mt 20:19 ("and
deliver him to the *ethnē* to be mocked and scourged and
crucified"), which is part of the third passion prediction, is
taken over from Mk 10:33 and also occurs in Lk 18:32. The
meaning of *ethnē* here is clearly (as Mt 20:18 shows) "Gentiles" and, more specifically, those Gentiles who carried out
the punishment and execution of criminals under the
Roman authorities in Jerusalem. The context of Mt 20:25
("the rulers of the *ethnē* lord it over them") is Jesus' rebuke
to the sons of Zebedee whose mother is seeking high places
for them in the kingdom. The same phrase occurs in Mk
10:42 and Lk 22:25, and the meaning of *ethnē* is "Gentiles."
The phrase "*ethnos* will rise against *ethnos*" occurs in Mt 24:7
as well as Mk 13:8 and Lk 21:10. If this prophecy is a
vaticinium ex eventu (at least for Matthew), it may well
include Israel. Here *ethnos* retains the original meaning as a
national group or collective. But this use of the word in the
singular here cannot be construed as decisive evidence that
the plural must have the same meaning for Matthew. Furthermore, the phrase has the ring of an apocalyptic cliché.

Two more texts must be mentioned at this point. Into a
saying found in Mk 13:13 and Lk 21:17 ("you will be hated
by all for my sake") Matthew in 24:9 has inserted *ethnē*. His
expression *'ypo pantōn tōn ethnōn* could include Israel, but
this interpretation is by no means necessary (see section 3

for further discussion). Mt 6:32 ("the *ethnē* seek all these things") occurs in that part of the Sermon on the Mount that deals with anxieties regarding food, drink, and clothing. The version in Lk 12:30 ("all the *ethnē* of the world") suggests that Matthew's form is probably closer to that of Q. At any rate, *ta ethnē* in Mt 6:32 refers to the Gentiles. Therefore, in the five instances of *ethnos/ethnē* where Matthew depends on the Marcan or the Q tradition, there are three (20:19, 25; 6:32) where it definitely means "Gentiles" and two (24:7, 9) where it *may* include Israel. These two instances, however, are not at all decisive.

The term *ethnos/ethnē* occurs nine times in material that is peculiar to Matthew. Since it is difficult and often impossible to distinguish between tradition and redaction in this material, we will treat all the instances together in order of their appearance in the Gospel. The phrase *Galilaia tōn ethnōn* in Mt 4:15 is part of the citation of Isa 9:1-2 (8:23— 9:1 in the MT) and translates the Hebrew *glyl hgwym;* it describes Galilee as inhabited by Gentiles. Mt 10:5 ("Go nowhere among the *ethnē*) is placed at the beginning of the so-called "missionary discourse" and is part of Jesus' advice to the Twelve to limit their mission to the lost sheep of Israel and not to go *eis 'odōn ethnōn.* Again, the meaning is "Gentiles." In Mt 10:18 ("and you will be dragged before governors and kings for my sake, to bear testimony before them and the *ethnē*") the sufferings of the disciples, inflicted by both Jews and Gentiles, will serve as a witness to the Gentiles. Two instances ("and he shall proclaim justice to the *ethnē*. . . and in his name will the *ethnē* hope") appear in the citation of Isa 42:1-4. In Mt 12:18 *ethnē* translates *gwym,* but in 12:21 it is used for *'yym* ("coastlands, islands"). In both cases *ethnē* must refer to nations other than Israel, and in their Matthean context both probably describe individual non-Jews. The saying in Mt 21:43 ("the kingdom of God will be taken away from you and given to an *ethnos* producing the fruits of it") comes at the end of the parable of wicked husbandmen and aims to draw a contrast between Israel and that new collective, the church, which is composed indiscriminately of Jews and Gentiles who receive the preaching of the kingdom and act upon it. In Mt 24:14 ("And this gospel of the kingdom will be preached throughout the whole world, as a testimony to all the *ethnē*") the phrase *pasin tois ethnesin* could conceivably include Israel, but some contrast between Israel and the whole world is implied (see section 3 for further discussion). In Mt 25:32 ("Before him will be gathered *panta ta ethnē*, and he will separate them") the phrase occurs in the parable of the last judgment. It could include Israel, but the parable is better interpreted in our view as responding to the question: By what criterion will the Gentiles who do not know Jesus be judged? That criterion turns out to be acts of love shown to "the least of these my brothers." According to this interpretation (see section 3 for further discussion) *panta ta ethnē* means "all the Gentiles." Before we approach what is our focal text (Mt 28:19), we should observe that for the eight uses of *ethnos/ethnē* in material peculiar to Matthew the obvious meaning in six (4:15; 10:5, 18; 12:18, 21; 21:43) is "Gentiles." In the other two texts (24:14; 25:32) *ethnē* could include Israel, but in both cases the interpretation as "Gentiles" seems preferable. Now when we come to Mt 28:19, the least we can say is that when Matthew uses *ethnos/ethnē* he usually means "Gentiles." But we believe that we must go further and say that he always means "Gentiles." If this is so, *mathēteusate panta ta ethnē* must mean "make disciples of all the Gentiles." Matthew does not envision the conversion of Israel as a nation; the time for that has passed. His Gospel reflects the conditions of a period in which the split between Israel and the church is definitive.[7]

---

[7]A much more detailed study of each instance of *ethnē* and *panta ta ethnē* in Mt can now be found in J. Lange's *Das Erscheinen des Auferstandenen im Evangelium nach Matthäus. Eine traditions- und redaktionsgeschichtliche Untersuchung zu Mt 28, 16-20* (Forschung zur Bibel 11; Würzburg: Echter, 1973) 248-305. His conclusions are fundamentally the same as those reached in our paper: "Matthew's universalism seems to be a universalism without Israel and over against Israel (*ohne Israel, gegen Israel*), which has betrayed and so lost its role and function in the circle of nations (270; see also 302)." K. W. Clark in *JBL* 66 (1947) 166 found evidence in this stance that the first Gospel was written by a Gentile, since no Jew

3. *The Case for* panta ta ethnē *Including Israel*

The most extensive recent defense of *panta ta ethnē* in Mt
28:19 as including Israel has been made by W. Trilling.[8] He
limits his examination to the four Matthean passages (24:9,
14; 25:32; 28:19) where *panta ta ethnē* occurs, without providing any explanation of this restriction. But are not all
instances of *ethnos/ethnē* in Mt pertinent? Trilling is aware
that for Matthew *ethnē* means non-Jews and sometimes
pagans,[9] but he apparently assumes that *ethnē* changes in
force when combined with *panta* and becomes a designation
for all mankind, Jewish as well as non-Jewish.

The key argument in defense of Trilling's view is that
25:32 ("Before him will be gathered *panta ta ethnē,* and he
will separate them") must refer to all nations including
Israel: "For Matthew it is a matter of the universal world
judgment of the Old Testament, which allows for no limita-
tion or differentiation among groups of persons."[10] But, in
fact, there is no uniform view of the OT of a universal
judgment addressed to all humans as individuals. The post-
resurrection judgment in Dan 12:2 involves "many (*rabbîm*)
of those who sleep in the dust of the earth." The prevalent
view seems to be that the *gôyîm* will be judged on the day of
the Lord in regard to their treatment of Israel (Joel 3[4 in
MT] and Ezek 39). This hint of two judgments, one for the
Gentiles and another for Israel, is picked up in intertestamental literature. In *2 Apoc. Bar.* 72 the bright lightning of
the cloud vision of chap. 53 is seen as referring to the
messiah's judging of the non-Jewish nations. In *Ps. Sol.*

would show such an anti-Jewish bias. But we feel that Matthew was a Jew whose
attitude can be explained as stemming from the zeal frequently displayed by
converts and from his church's desire to define itself over against the familiar but
now unacceptable Judaism of the synagogues.

[8]W. Trilling, *Das wahre Israel. Studien zu einer Theologie des Matthäusevange-
liums* (3d ed., SANT; Munich: Kösel, 1964) 26-28. Trilling's view has been adopted
by B. J. Hubbard, *The Matthean Redaction of a Primitive Apostolic Commissioning: An Exegesis of Matthew 28:16-20* (SBLDS 19; Missoula, Mont.: SBL and
Scholars' Press, 1974) 84-87.

[9]*Ibid.,* 115, 128.

[10]*Ibid.,* 27.

17:27-28 the judgment of the Gentiles precedes that of Israel. In the interpretation of the vision of the Man from the Sea in *4 Ezra* 13:33-49 the multitude gathered from the four winds represents the nations, and the peaceable multitude consists of the ten lost tribes of Israel. *1 Enoch* 90:20-27 presents a series of three judgments: the stars (fallen angels), the seventy shepherds (apparently angelic rulers who proved unfaithful),[11] and the blinded sheep (apostate Jews). *1 Enoch* 91:12-15 likewise depicts a threefold judgment: in the eighth week upon oppressors and sinners, in the ninth week on the godless of all the world, and in the tenth week on the angels. Finally and most explicitly, the Armenian text of *Test. Benj.* 10:8-9 states: "Then shall we all be changed, some into glory and some into shame; for the Lord judges Israel first for the unrighteousness which they have committed. And then so (shall he judge) all the Gentiles." The Armenian may well be transmitting to us the Jewish *Vorlage*.[12] The Greek and Slavonic versions add some obviously Christian material here, and "all the Gentiles" is *panta ta ethnē*. But even if the Armenian here is of Christian origin, this text would still reflect at least an early Christian belief in separate judgments for Israel and the Gentiles and presents a use of *panta ta ethnē* that clearly excludes the Jews.

There are also some hints in the NT that the final judgment involves different groups in different ways. In 1 Pet 4:17 judgment is said to begin with the household of God and to end with the godless. According to 1 Cor 6:2-3 the saints are to judge the world and the angels; this seems to presuppose a prior judgment for Christians, in which "the saints" are separated from the "pseudo-saints" (see 2 Cor 5:10). Rom 2:9-10 provides the clearest indication of separate judgments for Jews and Gentiles: "There will be tribulation and distress for every human being who does evil, the

---

[11]See R. H. Charles in *APOT II* 255 (note on *1 Enoch* 89:59).

[12]J. Becker, *Untersuchungen zur Entstehungsgeschichte der Testamente der zwölf Patriarchen* (AGJU 8: Leiden; Brill; 1970) 48-49. But for another view see M. de Jonge, "Christian Influence in the Testaments of the Twelve Patriarchs," *NovT* 4 1960) 229.

Jew first and also the Greek, but glory and honor and peace for everyone who does good, the Jew first and also the Greek." Even more relevant to our present study is the declaration in Mt 19:28 that Jesus' disciples will sit on twelve thrones to judge the twelve tribes of Israel. Regardless of how *krinein* is interpreted, this statement indicates that Jews will be treated as a special category distinct from the rest of mankind in the eschatological drama.

The point of gathering all these texts in the previous two paragraphs is to prove *contra* Trilling that Matthew need not have seen the judgment described in Mt 25:31-46 as applying to all human beings—Jews, Christians, and pagans. In our view it is more probable that Matthew understands the narrative as involving non-Christian Gentiles only who cannot be judged on the same basis as Jews (see Mt 19:28) or Christians (see 7:24-27; 10:32-33; 18:5, 18, 35). The passage assumes that those being judged had no direct contact with Jesus, either positive or negative ("Lord, when did we see thee . . ." 25:37). The thrust of the pericope is not simply that good deeds will receive an eschatological reward, but that the righteous of the pagan world have indeed formed a relationship with Jesus by their acts of love toward "the least" with whom he has identified himself.[13]

Trilling's arguments that the Jews are included among *panta ta ethne* in 24:9 and 14 are also not convincing. Matthew's addition of *tōn ethnōn* in 24:9 to Mk 13:13, which has only *'ypo pantōn,* is superfluous unless he intends to change the force of the Marcan phrase. One cannot explain the alteration except by assuming that Matthew intends to make the prediction apply to the hatred shown by Gentiles to Christians. He is not "nationalizing" the hatred ("you will be hated by the Roman nation, the Egyptian

[13]The traditional interpretation involves an exceptional expansion of *adelphoi* whereby it means "all the afflicted and needy"; see J. Jeremias, *The Parables of Jesus* (New York: Scribner's, 1963) 207. But Matthew may have intended *adelphoi* to describe Christians living in the pagan world; see W.D. Davies, *The Setting of the Sermon on the Mount* (Cambridge: Cambridge University Press, 1964) 98. Or he may have understood *adelphoi* as the disciples sent to the nations to preach the kingdom; see L. Cope, "Matthew xxv 31-46. 'The Sheep and the Goats' Reinterpreted," *NovT* 11 (1969) 32-44.

nation, etc."), but he is speaking to the experience of Christians in the non-Jewish world in the context of the Gentile mission. Nor is there any cogency in T. Zahn's argument, cited by Trilling,[14] that the Jewish nation is included in 24:14 among "all the nations" who are to receive the gospel, since the phrase *'ole tē oikoumenē* must include Palestine. The assumption underlying 24:14 (and Mk 13:10) is that the Jewish nation in Palestine has *already* heard the gospel. "To the Jew first, and also to the Greek" is Matthew's order (see Mt 10:5, 17-18) as well as Paul's (see Rom 1:16).

This examination of all the instances of *panta ta ethnē* in Matthew's Gospel apart from 28:19 reveals that in no case can it be persuasively argued that the phrase includes Israel. Rather, *panta ta ethnē* designates non-Jewish mankind in its entirety (with or without Gentile Christians).

4. *"Jews" and "Gentiles" in Matthean Theology*

We might accept the hypothesis that the use of *panta ta ethnē* in Mt 28:19 is exceptional, if it could be shown that Matthew's primary concern was historical accuracy. Then the post-resurrection mission to Israel would have to be included in the risen Lord's concluding commission. But such is not Matthew's concern. In Mt 10 he devotes a great amount of space to instructing the Twelve prior to their Galilean mission, but then omits any mention of the mission itself and the return. He does this because his interest is not in the pre-resurrection preaching tour but rather in the failure of the post-resurrection evangelistic activity in Israel. This same interest in the post-resurrection mission and its failure is also reflected in Mt 23:34-39; 5:10-12 and 22:6.[15]

---

[14]Trilling, *Das wahre Israel,* 28. The closest extra-Matthean parallel to the use of *panta ta ethnē* in Mt 28:19 is provided by Lk 24:47: ". . . and that repentance and forgiveness of sins should be preached in his name to *panta ta ethnē,* beginning from Jerusalem." Since Jerusalem is mentioned, Israel might be considered as part of *panta ta ethnē.* But Luke regularly employs *ethnē* to designate non-Jews. In fact, the dangling participle may be better taken with Lk 24:48 where it no longer dangles: "Beginning from Jerusalem, you are witnesses of these things" (cf. *NEB*).

[15]Hare, *The Theme of Jewish Persecution,* 80-129.

For Matthew this failure was foreordained (13:11-15); Israel's rejection of God and his Messiah has resulted in God's rejection of Israel (21:43; 22:7-8; 23:38).[16] Although the divine plan required that the gospel be preached first to the Jews (10:5; see 15:24, 26), for Matthew the time of the mission to Israel as Israel is over. The missionaries of the gospel have been subjected to judicial floggings (10:17; 23:34) and have been harried from town to town (10:23; 23:34).[17] Christians of Jewish origin no longer belong in "their synagogues" (4:23; 9:35; 10:17; 12:9; 13:54), which are the synagogues of the hypocrites (6:2,5; 23:6, 34).[18] For Matthew the twofold mission agreed upon by Paul and the "pillar" apostles at Jerusalem some three decades earlier (see Gal 2:7-9) has now been replaced by a single one. Henceforth, the mission is to the Gentiles: "Go, therefore, and make disciples of all the Gentiles . . ."

5. Some Patristic Interpretations of Mt 28:19

Although there are many allusions to Mt 28:19 in early Christian literature,[19] in most instances there is no mention of Israel in the context, so that we cannot determine whether the author understood *panta ta ethnē* as including or excluding Israel. But in those few passages where the Great Commission and Israel are mentioned together, *ethnē* seems to refer exclusively to the Gentiles. When commenting on Mt 13:57, Origen writes:

> And the apostles on this account left Israel and did that which had been enjoined on them by the Savior, "Make disciples of *panta ta ethnē*" and "You shall be my wit-

[16] *Ibid.,* 149-56.

[17] *Ibid.,* 92, 104-05.

[18] *Ibid.,* 104-05. See also G.D. Kilpatrick, *The Origins of the Gospel According to St. Matthew* (Oxford: Clarendon Press, 1946) 110-11.

[19] The Vetus Latina and the Vulgate of Mt 28:19 have *omnes gentes,* but *gentes* can mean both "nations" and "Gentiles" and is used in passages such as Gal 2:12 where only "Gentiles" is possible. The Peshitta uses '*mm*' to translate *ethnē* in Mt 28:19 as well as in 25:32 where it agrees with the Curetonian manuscript, but '*mm*' is also used in Gal 2:12.

nesses both in Jerusalem and in all Judea and Samaria, and to the uttermost part of the earth." For they did that which had been commanded them in Judea and Jerusalem; but since a prophet has no honor in his own country, when the Jews did not receive the Word, they went away to the *ethnē*.[20]

Eusebius shows a similar understanding of Mt 28:19, which he cites frequently in his *Demonstratio Evangelica*. The following text represents his viewpoint:

And since the Word predicted that the prophet would be raised up for them of the Circumcision, our Lord and Savior, being himself the one foretold, rightly said: "I am not come but to the lost sheep of the house of Israel." And he commanded his apostles, saying: "Go not into the road of the Gentiles, and into any city of the Samaritans enter ye not, but rather go to the lost sheep of the house of Israel" showing clearly that he was primarily sent to them as the prophecy required. But when they would not receive his grace, he reproves them elsewhere, saying: "For I came and there was no man, I called and there was none that heard." And he says to them: "The kingdom of God shall be taken away from you and shall be given to a nation bearing the fruits of it." And he bids his own disciples after their rejection: "Go and make disciples of *panta ta ethnē* in my name." So, then, we that are *ethnē* know and receive the prophet that was foretold . . . while the Jewish nation (*ethnos*), not receiving him that was foretold . . . has paid the fit penalty . . . .[21]

John Chrysostom in his homily on Jn 17:1-5 says:

---

[20]Origen, *PG* 13, 881. Quoted with minor changes from *Ante-Nicene Fathers* 10, 426.

[21]Eusebius, *PG* 22, 692-693. Quoted with minor changes from W. F. Ferrar, *The Proof of the Gospel, Being the Demonstratio Evangelica of Eusebius of Caesarea* II (London: SPCK, 1920) 175-76. This reference occurs in section 445 of the *Demonstratio;* other references to our text are in sections 6, 9, 24, 132, 136, 138. See also *Historia Ecclesiastica* 3.5.2.

For then he (Jesus) said: "Go not into the road of the *ethnē.*" But afterwards he would say: "Go, make disciples of *panta ta ethnē"* and declare that the Father also wills this. This scandalized the Jews very much and even the disciples.[22]

Conclusion

At the very least, those who maintain the inclusive interpretation of Mt 28:19 must concede that if Matthew intended to convey the idea "all nations, including Israel," his choice of expression was unfortunate. The plural *ethnē,* with or without *panta,* normally means non-Jews in Jewish and Christian writings and especially in Matthew's Gospel. A mission charge that included Israel would have been better indicated by *mathēteusate pantas tous laous* (see Lk 2:31).[23] Moreover, since the verb *mathēteuein* would normally apply to individuals, not to national collectives (whether *ethnē* or *laoi*), one must ask why Matthew did not simply use *pantas* if he thought that the commission included Israel (see Rom 11:32). Instead he chose to use *ethnē,* the equivalent of *gôyîm* for Greek-speaking Jews and a designation for "foreigners" in non-Jewish Greek.[24] The choice was surely deliberate. He meant "make disciples of all the Gentiles."[25]

Douglas R. A. Hare   *Daniel J. Harrington, S.J.*

[22]John Chrysostom, *PG* 59, 433-434.

[23]In the Apocalypse *ethnē* sometimes retains its corporate meaning of "nations" when combined with other collectives (*laois* 10:11; *ochloi* 17:15; cf. the frequent collocation of the singular *ethnos* with *laos, phylē* and/ or *glōssa,* 5:9; 7:9; 10:11; 11:9; 13:7; 14:6; 17:15), but in such collocations, both singular and plural, the context suggests that the reference is to non-Jewish groups.

[24]For this connotation as "foreigners" in secular Greek see W. Bauer, *A Greek-English Lexicon of the New Testament and Other Early Christian Literature* (rev. and tr. W.F. Arndt and F.W. Gingrich; Chicago: University of Chicago, 1957) 217. It is interesting to note that H. Rackham in the Loeb translation of Aristotle's *Politics* 1324b translates *en tois ethnesi pasin* as "among all the non-Hellenic nations."

[25]We must express our gratitude to our fellow members of the CBA Task Force on Matthew (J. A. Comber, L. Cope, J. D. Kingsbury, J. P. Meier, J. M. Reese, and W. G. Thompson) for encouraging and criticizing our work on this topic during the sessions held at the 1974 meeting of the CBA in Chicago.

7. CHURCH AND MINISTRY

1. What is the significance of biblical statements about the church for Christians today?

Christians today must respect the variety of theological voices within the canon of Scripture and the historical nature of the NT documents. Moreover, they must recognize that there is no single, all-embracing pattern emerging out of Scripture to which the church must adhere. Nevertheless, the apostolic era is a privileged period in Christian history, and the statements about the church in its documents have provided direction and challenge throughout the centuries. The church is headed in the right direction when the preaching of Jesus and the response to it found in the NT serve as its most basic criteria.

2. Is the church the same as the kingdom of God?

No. The fullness of God's kingdom is future. It is God's reign, and it is up to him to bring about a new heaven and a new earth. The present or inaugurated aspect of the kingdom of God resides in the person of Jesus, not directly in the church. The church is the community of those who believe in Jesus and his preaching of the kingdom. It preserves that preaching and tries to be faithful to it, lives its life against the horizon of the kingdom, and is the sign of hope for the kingdom in the future.

3. Did Jesus found the church?

The origin of the church lies in the entire action of God in Jesus Christ. The most decisive moment in that action was the resurrection when God raised up the crucified one and poured out the Spirit upon the disciples. God is the true founder of the church in that he calls together those who believe in the risen Lord and look for the coming kingdom. Certain features of Jesus' earthly ministry (e.g. preaching the kingdom, sharing meals, showing a free attitude toward the Law, gathering a circle of disciples) furnished a basis for the emergence of the church after Easter. Nevertheless, the primary task of the earthly Jesus was proclaiming the reign of God, not establishing an ecclesiastical institution.

4. Has the discovery of the Dead Sea scrolls aided our understanding of the earliest church?

The Qumran scrolls, which were found near the Dead Sea shortly after the Second World War, provide first-hand information about a Palestinian-Jewish, eschatologically-oriented community contemporary with earliest Christianity. While there is no evidence of a direct relationship between the Qumran community and the Jerusalem church (insofar as it can be known from Acts 1-7), they had many features in common: focus on the day of the Lord, concern with the meaning of the OT and its fulfillment in the present, and practices of piety (ritual washings, common meals, community of goods, etc.).

5. What is the decisive difference between the Qumran sect and the Jerusalem church?

Faith in the power of the death and resurrection of Jesus set the early church apart from the Qumran sect. For Christians, the complex of eschatological events had been put in motion through Jesus and the Scriptures had been brought to completion in him. Also, the Jerusalem church was urban and missionary in contrast to the quasi-monastic pattern of life observed by the Qumran sect.

6. What did Christian baptism have in common with ritual washings of the time, and what was distinctive about it?

To be baptized meant to be dipped down or immersed in water. The Qumran community had a very elaborate system of ritual washings and a keen interest in ritual purification. But the baptism of John is the chief analogue for Christian baptism in that it apparently took place only once and was concerned with moral purity in preparation for the eschatological judgment. What was distinctive about Christian baptism was the fact that it was done "in the name of Jesus Christ." Christian baptism was not only preparation for the eschatological judgment but also the appropriation in the present of the salvation proclaimed by and in Jesus Christ.

7. What did the Christian Eucharist have in common with rites of the time, and what was distinctive about it?

The Qumran community celebrated a regular common meal at which a priest presided (see 1QS 6:2-5), and this was understood as the anticipation of the messianic banquet to take place at the end of time (see 1QSa 2:17-22). Regular common meals were also a prominent feature of the Pharisaic movement. What was distinctive about the communal meals of the Christians was the direct connection to Jesus Christ. The Christian Eucharist recalled the death of Jesus, celebrated his resurrection and presence through the Spirit, and looked toward the heavenly banquet of the future.

8. What social position did the NT communities have?

In the Jewish world and especially in the pagan world, the Christians constituted a distinct minority. Outsiders viewed them as unnecessary and even dangerous, and the Christians described themselves as "aliens and exiles" (1 Pet 2:11; see also Heb 11:13). Any chance of direct political involvement or influence was out of the question. Early Christians considered the present social order as a passing phenomenon and encouraged each other to give good example in order to win more people to Christ.

9. Has Israel been definitively rejected as God's people?

Not according to Paul in Romans 9-11. While part of Israel rejected the gospel, some Israelites like Paul himself embraced it. The partial Jewish rejection of the gospel inspired the Gentile mission, and the Gentile mission will eventually make the rest of Israel so jealous that it will finally accept the gospel. The partial hardening of Israel is viewed by Paul as providential, and all Israel will be saved in the end. A church without any relation to Israel was unthinkable for Paul.

10. How are the negative comments about the Jews in the Gospels of Matthew and John to be interpreted?

Both Gospels were written fifteen or twenty years after the destruction of the Jerusalem Temple in A.D. 70. The catastrophic event caused all Jews to examine how the religious heritage of Israel could be handed on. With their negative portrayals of the scribes and Pharisees as Jesus' opponents, the Evangelists were attempting to define the Christian community as the true Israel over against the rival claims of the synagogues. Since many in the Matthean and Johannine communities were Christian Jews, the term "anti-Semitism" is hardly applicable. Unlike Paul, neither Evangelist had much interest in the future of Israel as an entity in salvation history.

11. What does the term "church" mean in the NT?

The word for church is *ekklēsia*. While in the Greek world it referred to a regularly summoned political body and had no religious connotation, in the Greek version of the OT known as the Septuagint it was used to describe the congregation of Israelites chosen by God and gathered around him for religious purposes. By taking over the term *ekklēsia* the primitive Christian community made the claim to be the true congregation of God after the pattern of the OT people of God. In the NT *ekklēsia* can refer to the local Christian community (the far more common usage) or to the universal church to which all believers belong (especially in Ephesians).

12. Granted that for Paul the local community was the church, were there universalistic dimensions to his theology and practice?

Paul's theology was shaped by a universalistic outlook; e.g., belief in the God of Israel as the only true God, conviction that all humanity needs salvation (see Rom 1:18—3:31), faith in the worldwide significance of Christ, and the understanding of the church as the totality of those redeemed in Christ. Paul's missionary practice had ecumenical dimensions; e.g., preaching Christ only where the gospel had not been heard, communicating with various local churches by emissaries and letters, and taking up the collection for the Jerusalem church (see Rom 15:25-27; 1 Cor 16:1-4).

13. What is new about the church in Ephesians?

Most modern interpreters view Ephesians as an essay written by a Jewish-Christian admirer of Paul around A.D. 80. The author is concerned with the church as an entity above and beyond the local communities (see 1:22; 3:21; 5:24). The church as the new unity of humanity is a central theme, not merely a corollary of Christology as in Paul's letters. The apostles and prophets are viewed as the foundation of the church (see 2:20), and stress is placed on the teaching charisms as guaranteeing sound doctrine (see 4:11, 14). The unity between Christ and the church is described in terms of head/body and husband/wife.

14. Is there more than one image for the church in the NT?

Yes. The most important images are the people of God, the community led by the Spirit, the charismatic community, the body of Christ, the temple of God, the saints, the flock, and the vine and the branches. The various images are presented obliquely in the course of resolving practical problems, and no document (unless it be Ephesians) takes as its central theme the nature of the church. The images cluster around two recurrent themes: the church as an historical entity standing in continuity with the OT people of

God, and the church as the place in which the power of the risen Lord and his Spirit are manifested. Far from being competitors, these two themes are often present in the same NT book. In dealing with the so-called models of the church, it is a matter of emphasis, not of choosing one to the exclusion of the others.

15. How is the church the people of God?

The identification of the church as the people of God is made explicitly only in 1 Pet 2:9-10, but it is surely the background for many other NT texts. Insofar as Christ has fulfilled the hopes of the OT people of God, those gathered around him—whether they be of Jewish or Gentile origin—constitute the true people of God. The church retains the same structure of faith as Israel in the OT (divinely initiated, historical, covenantal) and has been granted the prerogatives of the OT people of God. Those who accept Jesus Christ are bound together in a unity so close that the terms "chosen race, royal priesthood, holy nation, God's own people" (1 Pet 2:9) are entirely appropriate. As the wandering people of God (see Heb 3:7—4:11; 11:13-16), they must learn from Israel's bad example of disobedience and remain faithful while seeking rest with God in the heavenly place where Christ acts as high priest.

16. How is the church the community of the Holy Spirit?

According to Paul, the present manifestation of the freedom won for us by Christ (see Romans 1—8) is life in the Holy Spirit. Each and every Christian is a bearer of the Holy Spirit, and the presence of the Spirit demands a response shown in fitting behavior. The present manifestations of the Spirit are the first-fruits or pledge of the coming kingdom of God. According to John, the force sustaining the community in the absence of the earthly Jesus is the Paraclete or Spirit of truth (see John 14:15-17; 14:26; 15:26; 16:7-11) who teaches, bears witness to Jesus, and convicts the world of sin.

17. How is the church a charismatic community?

The term *charisma* ("gift") refers to the unfolding of Christ's power within individual Christians in the context of the church's life. In Rom 12:3-8 (see also 1 Cor 12) Paul insists that each Christian is a gifted person, that there is a variety of gifts or charisms, that these are the individuation of grace (*charis*), and that they are to be used in the service of the community. Charisms are directed toward the service of the whole community, not for the recipient's glorification. These manifestations of the Spirit must be consistent with the confession of Jesus as Lord (1 Cor 12:3), must be motivated by and carried out in love (1 Cor 13), and must build up the community (1 Cor 14:3, 4, 5, 12, 17, 26).

18. How is the church the body of Christ?

The local Christian community is the body of Christ (see 1 Cor 12:27) insofar as it is the means by which Christ reveals himself on earth and becomes incarnate in the world through the Spirit. The experience of the Spirit in baptism is fundamental for becoming a member of the body of Christ. The body does not come into existence solely through the decision of like-minded and interested persons. Rather, the Spirit as the vital principle of the body makes incorporation possible. Fellowship (*koinōnia*) is first and foremost a relationship to Christ ("the body of Christ") and only consequently a relationship to other believers.

19. How is the church the temple of God?

The criticism of the temple at Jerusalem in Acts 7 and in Hebrews is exceptional in the NT, and usually the emphasis falls on consideration of what is new rather than on what is old. The church as God's temple (see 1 Cor 3:16; 2 Cor 6:16; Eph 2:21) possesses the gift of the divine presence and a God-derived stability and order mediated by Christ. These gifts constitute a call to holiness and sacrificial living.

20. How are Christians called "the saints"?

The eschatological notion of the saints as the elect who will share in the blessing of the messianic kingdom provides the background for the NT use of this designation for Christians. The saints of the NT (see Rom 12:13; 15:25; 1 Cor 1:2; 2 Cor 9:1; etc.) are the holy community constituted by Christ and composed of those who have been chosen and called by God to a future inheritance. This community is meant to be distinguished by moral purity and goodness.

21. What are the most distinctive Johannine images for the church?

In John 10:1-18 those who belong to Jesus are the sheep-fold whose gate is Christ (vv. 1-10) and the flock whose shepherd is Christ (vv. 11-18). Discipleship demands recognizing the voice of the shepherd and responding to it. In John 15:1-5 the disciples are related to Christ as branches are related to the vine. Discipleship entails abiding in the vital relationship and demands fruitfulness.

22. How is leadership to be exercised in the NT communities?

Leadership is service (*diakonia*). Early Christianity made a conscious effort to redefine authority by rejecting existing patterns of leadership in Jewish and Greco-Roman society and by making the pattern of Christ the servant (see Mark 10:35-45; Phil 2:6-11) the ideal and the measure of Christian leadership. Christian leaders (see 1 Tim 3:1-13; 5:17-25; 2 Tim 2:22-25; Tit 1:5-9) are to be people of deep faith in God, to be aware that their own achievements are the gifts of the Spirit, and to show a willingness to work hard and even suffer for others.

23. Is shared responsibility a NT perspective?

Yes. In Acts the community shares in major decisions such as the election of Matthias (1:23-26), the appointment of the Seven (6:1-6), and the "council" of Jerusalem (15). In his letters Paul advises the communities but does not make formal decisions for them (see 1 Cor 5:1-5). In Matthew 18 the Christian community is an assembly of "brothers" and shares in the power of binding and loosing (see 18:18). In the primitive church important decisions were not made apart from the consent of the community. Even with the emergence of the "monarchical" episcopate the cooperation of the whole community was considered indispensable for the life of the church.

24. What was the most basic form of ministry in the NT?

Ministry in the NT was primarily ministry of the word in its various forms. In the lists of charisms (see Rom 12:6-8; 1 Cor 12:28-31; Eph 4:11) there is great emphasis on communicating the word or the good news of salvation as an important way of serving the community. 1 Thes 2:1-16 provides Paul's autobiographical reflection on being a minister of the word and gives us a glimpse of what this meant in the lives of individuals. Paul recognized himself as an instrument of God's power, did not act for personal gain or comfort, aroused considerable opposition, and preached the good news about what God had done in the death and resurrection of Jesus Christ. Paul's respect for traditional summaries of faith (see 1 Cor 15:1-11) and his use of terms like "the gospel of God" and "the word of God" indicates that the word to be preached had an objective character. Faithful to the core of Christian faith, Paul sought to articulate for his people the true significance of the gospel with respect to their problems.

25. Did Jesus exercise an official ministry within Judaism?

No. Jesus acted as a healer, preacher, and teacher without official ordination or authoritative human approval. There is no indication that he was trained under a rabbi, nor was he born into a priestly family. According to the criteria of Judaism in his time, Jesus did not hold a religious office.

26. What roles did bishops, deacons, and presbyters play in the early church?

While there are passing references to these offices in the early Pauline epistles (see Phil 1:1) and Acts, only the Pastoral epistles (see 1 Tim 3:1-13; 5:17-25; Tit 1:5-9) provide specific information about qualifications and functions. The Pastorals, which were most likely composed between A.D. 80 and 90 by an admirer of Paul, bear witness to the increasing emphasis on locally based officials for safeguarding the deposit of faith and defending against false doctrine. The precise relationship between bishops and deacons on the one hand and the presbyters on the other hand is not clear in the Pastorals. But in the letters of Ignatius of Antioch (martyred at Rome in A.D. 108) the single bishop clearly was the pivotal figure in the local church, had authority over the presbytery (the collective of elders) and the deacons, and had jurisdiction over the administration of the sacraments.

27. What was the significance of the imposition of hands?

The issue is debated. The imposition of hands (see 1 Tim 4:14; 2 Tim 1:6; Acts 13:3) may refer to a blessing or to a transfer of authority. If the blessing interpretation is accepted, then the imposition of hands means conferring a blessing and petitioning for the divine favor. If the transfer interpretation is held on the analogy of rabbinic ordination, then the idea is creating a substitute and sending that person out on a mission.

28. Does the NT describe each and every Christian as a priest?

In the epistle to the Hebrews the term *hiereus* ("priest") applies only to Christ who fulfilled the OT notion of sacrifice and brought the Jewish cultic system to an end. Nowhere in the NT is *hiereus* used for someone who holds an office in the church. The term *hiereus* is applied to Christians in a few texts. The application in 1 Pet 2:9 is metaphorical and collective and is a way of describing the elect and holy character of God's people, not the rights and privileges of individuals. Rev 1:6; 5:10; 20:4-6 call redeemed Christians priests, but the eschatological character of this priesthood makes problematic its significance in the present time. Do the references in Revelation say that each baptized person is a priest, or do they use a metaphor to describe God's holy people?

29. How did the classic image of the Christian priest arise?

The term *hiereus* ("priest") could not be used of Christian ministers until separation from Judaism had become complete and definitive. Only in the last quarter of the second century A.D. did *hiereus* become a common designation for Christian office holders. This occurred as a corollary to the growing recognition of the Eucharist as a sacrifice: The one who presides at the eucharistic sacrifice is a priest. The classic image of the Christian priest fuses several different roles: disciple, apostle, presbyter-bishop, and president at the Eucharist.

30. What does it mean to call the church apostolic?

In the NT "apostle" is not a univocal term. While Paul saw the apostle as one sent by the risen Lord, Luke identified the apostles with the Twelve (plus Paul) and limited the term to those who accompanied the earthly Jesus. Other texts (see 2 Cor 8:23) see the apostle as an authorized missionary. Fundamental to these notions is the belief that the apostle is the instrument of the risen Lord until his glorious return and is charged with preaching the gospel under the guidance of the Spirit. The church is apostolic when it remains true to this belief and to the ministry of the apostles.

31. How is Peter portrayed in the NT?

Simon Peter was one of the first disciples called by Jesus and was the most prominent among the Twelve. He confessed Jesus as the Messiah (see Mark 8:27-33), but this confession reflected an incomplete understanding on his part. He was granted an appearance of the risen Lord (see 1 Cor 15:5; Luke 24:34), was the most important among the disciples in Jerusalem and environs, and had a missionary career ending in martyrdom in Rome. He is portrayed in the NT as the repentant sinner, the guardian of the faith, the recipient of a special revelation, the pastor or shepherd, and great fisherman (missionary). Recent scholarship establishes the promise to Peter in Mt 16:17-19 as a pre-Matthean tradition, but is divided as to its origin (the words of the earthly Jesus, a promise made during a post-resurrection appearance, or a legend about the founding apostle of the church at Antioch). Moreover, the perpetuity of the promise and the Roman character of the perpetuity are debated, frequently along denominational lines.

32. Were there female ministers in the NT church?

Women served as deacons (see Rom 16:1; 1 Tim 3:11) and prophets (Acts 21:9; 1 Cor 11:5; Rev 2:20), and early interpreters were not disturbed at the possibility that the apostle Junia(s) in Rom 16:7 might have been a woman. Women exercised an especially important role in the Pauline mission, but later texts like 1 Pet 3:1-7; 1 Tim 2:9-15; Tit 2:3-5 witness a reversion to acceptance of Jewish and Hellenistic cultural attitudes regarding the place of women. Ordination of women to the priesthood and the episcopacy today is more a matter of hermeneutics than of exegesis, of what the Bible means today than of what it says, since no woman is known to have held these offices in NT times.

33. How did the early church deal with post-baptismal sin?

Being part of the community of saints did not excuse Christians for being sinners. Examination of texts like Mt 16:19; 18:18; John 20:19-23; Jas 5:15-16; and 1 John 1:8-10 shows that sinners were expected to recognize their guilt, confess their sins, and reform themselves. The church excommunicated and lifted the ban; it retained and absolved sins. This was done under the authority of Jesus, who had given the church this power.

34. On what grounds were people excluded from the Christian communities?

Exclusion from the Christian community was used mainly as a penalty for moral offenses, the classic example being the case of the incestuous man in 1 Cor 5:1-5. Paul's anathema in Gal 1:8-9 pronounced against those who would pervert the gospel is the closest parallel to ecclesiastical excommunication for doctrinal reasons. While it is difficult to find an instance of formal excommunication for errors of faith, the natural interrelationship between ideas and actions and the warnings levelled against false teachers in the Pastorals, the Johannine letters, and Jude and 2 Peter do point in that direction.

35. In what sense are the NT churches one?

The unity of the NT churches resides in the unity of God. The one Spirit by whose power the one God reveals himself in the one Christ creates the one body of Christ which is the church. This unity is served by the one gospel, one baptism, one Eucharist, church offices, and various charisms (see Eph 4:1-6). The unity of the church is realized through faith, hope, and love, especially in the liturgical gatherings of the community. The continuing threat to unity and the experience of failure in realizing it are signs of our need for God's eschatological intervention.

8. GOD'S PEOPLE IN CHRIST: CHALLENGES FOR THE CHURCH TODAY

My book *God's People in Christ* presented a description of early Christianity's attempts at defining itself with reference to Judaism. Attention to representative Old Testament passages revealed some important dimensions of Israel's sense of being God's people: divinely initiated, historical, and covenantal. A glance at some postexilic texts showed that these ideas continued to exercise great influence, though special emphasis was placed on observing particular commandments or belonging to particular groups. In the context of belonging to God's people, Jesus of Nazareth preached about the future and present aspects of the kingdom. Those gathered around Jesus in life and death looked very much like other Jewish apocalyptic communities of their time but were distinguished from them primarily by faith in Jesus' death and resurrection as God's decisive intervention in human history.

Paul's position that "if you are Christ's, then you are Abraham's offspring" (Gal 3:29) constituted a major breakthrough. It encouraged those who were not born as Jews to share in the religious heritage of Israel by means of incorporation into Christ. Membership in God's people was now defined in religious rather than ethnic terms. In Romans 9—11 Paul argued that all who accept Christ in faith—whether they are Jews or Gentiles by origin—are the real children of Abraham. Nevertheless, he also saw a place within God's plan of salvation for those Israelites who did not yet profess faith in Christ. The author of Ephesians stressed that the people made up of Jews and Gentiles forms the body of Christ, that in and through Christ Jews and Gentiles have been shaped into a single people.

The other side of the "togetherness" in Christ so vigorously encouraged by Paul and the author of Ephesians was the tendency toward distinguishing the people of God in Christ from those Jews and Gentiles who were not in Christ. Some of the dynamics of this process appear in 1 Timothy: emphasis on sound doctrine, exemplary behavior as a missionary strategy, the idea of the church as God's household and the bulwark of truth, and the growing importance attached to church officials. The imagery connected with ancient Israel's sense of peoplehood was invoked by the authors of 1 Peter, Hebrews, and Revelation as a way of expressing the self-consciousness of the Christian community. The Gospels of Matthew and John reflect the struggles with other Jewish religious movements after A.D. 70 for the right to claim the heritage of Israel as God's own people.

Our biblical-theological investigation of the church as God's people in Christ has focused on specific texts in the hope of getting in touch with some decisive ecclesiological moments in the earliest stages of Christian history. The method has been exegetical and descriptive, and the result is a series of glimpses into some varieties of communal consciousness found in the biblical tradition. Perhaps other parts of the New Testament deserve further attention (for example, Luke-Acts),[1] and perhaps other aspects of the documents treated here (for example, the anti-Jewish char-

---

[1]G. Lohfink, *Die Sammlung Israels: Eine Untersuchung zur lukanischen Ekklesiologie* (SANT 39; Munich: Kösel, 1975).

acter of the passion stories in the Gospels)[2] merit further examination. But enough exegesis has been presented and a sufficient variety of insights have been explored to leave the reader at this point asking about the overall theological significance of the study.

What does it mean to call the church "the people of God"? What are the most important challenges to the church today that emerge out of the individual analyses presented in this book? I have no intention of gathering together all the relevant information about the church as the people of God and mixing it into one comprehensive doctrine of the church. Rather I will try to remain faithful to the thrusts of the particular texts studied here and will explore some of their ramifications for the life of the church today. After all, the Christian churches affirm that these biblical texts are authoritative in some way and therefore Christians take upon themselves the obligation to listen to the texts and act upon them. Indeed the statements about the church in the documents of the so-called apostolic period have furnished direction and vitality to the Christian community throughout the centuries. At a time in history when so many of the church's cultural moorings are being cut away and when people are legitimately concerned to know what is essential and what is accidental about the ways in which our churches operate, a serious reflection on the foundational documents of Christianity can only have a purifying and salutary effect. My concluding observations will be presented as a series of challenges to the church today that I think arise out of the biblical texts examined in *God's People in Christ*.

1. Israel's spiritual heritage. If the church is to carry on the spiritual heritage of the Old Testament people of God, it must see itself as graced and as called by God, must look to

[2]G. S. Sloyan, *Jesus on Trial: The Development of the Passion Narratives and Their Historical and Ecumenical Implications* (Philadelphia: Fortress Press, 1973). See also J.R. Donahue, *Are You the Christ? The Trial Narrative in the Gospel of Mark* (SBLDS 10; Cambridge, MA: Society of Biblical Literature, 1973).

the events of history as a place of divine revelation, and must remain faithful to the covenantal structure of faith. In Galatians 3 and Romans 4, Paul insists that through Christ even Gentiles can become children of Abraham and part of God's people. A corollary to this claim is the idea that Abraham is the model or pattern of genuine Christian faith. According to the stories about Abraham presented in the Old Testament and treasured by the early Christians, Abraham left his homeland in response to God's call to him. Abraham's vocation was not to individual salvation or to personal growth but rather to stand at the head of a people with a God, a land, and a law. The vivid sense of belonging to a people, of solidarity with others, of being part of something larger than oneself—all this is involved in the church's claim to be God's people in Christ. The Old Testament passages about the people of God do not claim this status for Israel because of Israel's own merits or its natural abilities or its size. God's grace, and not Israel's achievements, is at the root of the people's identity: "It is because the Lord loves you" (Deut 7:8). Likewise, the church's claim to be God's people must never degenerate into exclusionism or triumphalism, because whatever status it has before God is based entirely on God's initiative. Moreover, we saw that the Old Testament people of God looked upon the events of history, especially the Exodus from Egypt and the gift of the land of Canaan, as an arena for God's activity on its behalf. This same kind of commitment to think about and act upon the events of history from a religious point of view sustained the Jewish people through the triumphs and catastrophes of its later history and allowed the New Testament writers to discern in the life, death, and resurrection of Jesus of Nazareth God's most decisive intervention in human affairs. Whenever the church separates itself from the world in which it exists and pretends to have no interest in the events of its time, its claim to be God's people may be legitimately doubted. Finally, like Israel of old, the church stands in a covenant relationship with God. Recognizing the validity of God's claims over it, the church must seek to respond in ways that are appropriate to its identity as God's people in Christ. God's people in Christ as children of Abraham cannot neglect its spiritual roots and cannot avoid the challenges raised by the shape of Israel's peoplehood: the appreciation of God's grace, the obligation to discern the hand of God in our history, and the acknowledgment of God's covenantal lordship and of our status as his servants.

2. The centrality of Christ. The church's claim to be God's people is based entirely on the person of Jesus Christ. Jesus the Jew of Nazareth is the principle of continuity between Israel of old and the church. By confessing Jesus of Nazareth as the Messiah of Jewish expectation, the church affirms that it now carries on the Jewish spiritual heritage. Whereas the Qumran community saw the events involving its own group as the key that unlocked the mysteries of the Scriptures, early Christian interpreters like Luke, Paul, the author of Hebrews, and Matthew insisted that Christ is the key to the Scriptures. So impressed with Jesus Christ were the early Christians that they confessed him as the vehicle for the fulfillment of God's promises to Israel. By nature Jesus belonged to God's people Israel, and this one Israelite has made it possible for individuals of all ethnic backgrounds to be part of that people.

Are we not all God's people? Does not the mere fact of creation make us part of the people of God? Not exactly! When we use the term "the people of God," we refer to the mysterious special relationship existing between God and a certain segment of humanity that is the principal theme of the Bible. As I have previously emphasized, that special relationship is not based on merit or achievement but upon grace. If one accepts the Scriptures as authoritative documents, one also affirms that "a people of God" exists within the much larger expanse of humanity. The issue that confronted the early church was this: How do individuals enter that special relationship with God? The answer provided by Paul and those who followed his lead was that one enters the special communal relationship with God in and through

Jesus Christ. Jesus of Nazareth appears as the great principle of continuity for the people of God and as the means by
which all kinds of men and women "from every tribe and
tongue and people and nation" become part of God's people
in Christ.

What about those who are not part of God's people in
Christ in any conscious or explicit way? The New Testament
writers hoped for a time in which all people would recognize
the decisive significance of Christ within God's plan of
salvation. They viewed Christ as the savior of the people of
God and showed little interest in other possible ways of
salvation. This apparent insularity was due in large part to
early Christianity's eschatological orientation ("this world
is passing away") and to the narrow geographical outlook of
those who inhabited the lands around the Mediterranean
Sea at the turn of the common era. The idea of universal
salvation (universalism) is foreign to the New Testament,
but the notion that all who do not make an explicit profession of faith in Jesus Christ are condemned (damnationism)
is not championed either. The ultimate fate of nonbelievers
is left in the hands of God.[3] However, the references to the
cosmic significance of Christ's saving action in Paul's letters
(see 2 Cor 5:19; Rom 8:19-23; 11:15) and in the letters to the
Colossians (see 1:20; 2:10, 15) and the Ephesians (see 1:10,
20-22; 3:10) may furnish some New Testament foundation
for the inclusion within God's special people of those who
remain "anonymous Christians" (to use Karl Rahner's
somewhat infelicitous phrase).[4]

---

[3] J. A. Burgess, "Approaches to the Question of Universal Salvation on the Basis
of the New Testament," *Ohio Journal of Religious Studies* 5 (1977) 142-48.

[4] K. Rahner, "Anonymous Christians," in *Theological Investigations Volume
VI: Concerning Vatican Council II,* trans. K.-H. and B. Kruger (London: Darton,
Longman & Todd, 1969; New York: Seabury Press) 390-98. Rahner's effort at
grounding the idea of anonymous Christians in 1 Tim 2:4 ("who [God] desires all to
be saved and to come to the knowledge of the truth") prescinds from the fact that in
the Pastorals the expression "the knowledge of the truth" (see also 2 Tim 2:25; 3:7;
Tit 1:1) is a formula for Christianity; that is, conversion to the Christian faith. See
M. Dibelius and H. Conzelmann, *The Pastoral Epistles* (Hermeneia; Philadelphia:
Fortress Press, 1972) 41.

3. The communal significance of baptism. Baptism into Christ is the way by which we become part of God's people here and now. Many Jewish groups of Jesus' time practiced ritual washings of various sorts, but the distinctive feature about Christian baptism was its power to incorporate one into the body of Christ. In Rom 6:3-4 baptism is portrayed as identification with the decisive events of Christ's life: "Do you not know that all of us who have been baptized into Christ Jesus were baptized into his death? We were buried therefore with him by baptism into death, so that as Christ was raised from the dead by the glory of the Father, we too might walk in newness of life." Galatians 3 states that "as many of you as were baptized into Christ have put on Christ" (v. 27) and that being "Christ's" makes us Abraham's offspring and heirs according to the promise. The rite of baptism obviously presupposes faith in the decisive significance of Jesus' life, death, and resurrection.[5] Consideration of how all of us—whatever our ethnic origins—become part of God's people reminds us that faith in Christ holds us together and helps us to appreciate the seriousness of our baptism. The long-standing debate about the appropriateness of infant baptism may never be resolved, but that debate should not be carried on as if the only alternatives were the informed personal commitment that only an adult can give and the desire to "cleanse" the infant from original sin. The importance of belonging to the community of faith is a factor too, and the communal dimension of salvation that emerges from understanding the church as God's people in Christ must not be overlooked. Baptism into Christ makes us members of God's people in Christ.

4. Christians as "honorary Jews." The Jewish roots of our Christian faith must be celebrated and not denied. The structure of faith after the pattern of Abraham—divinely initiated, historical, covenantal—is normative for the

[5]D. J. Harrington, "Baptism in the Spirit: A Review Article," *Chicago Studies* 11 (1972) 31-44.

church. The Old Testament Scriptures must be proclaimed within the church, for they become fully intelligible according to Paul and the other New Testament authors only in the person of Jesus. In Romans 9—11 Paul shows that in a real sense we Gentile Christians are honorary Jews.[6] Paul could not conceive of the church as God's people in Christ without its having some relationship to Israel after the flesh. In the terms of Paul's parable, we Gentile Christians have been grafted onto the olive tree which is Israel. Even those New Testament books that engage in what is sometimes called "replacement theology" (that is, the church replaces Israel as God's people) exhibit a very serious interest in Israel's spiritual heritage. For example, the author of Hebrews takes the Exodus generation's wandering in the wilderness as a warning to the Christian community in 3:7—4:11, and the author of Revelation encourages his community in its crisis by reminding it of its status as priests of God. The church today cannot allow its Jewish past to be ignored, for without that past there is no validity to its claim to be God's people in Christ.

5. The scandal of anti-Semitism. The church must be on guard against anti-Semitism.[7] The church's claim to carry on the spiritual heritage of Israel has all too often provided individuals and groups with "theological" justifications for persecuting those Jews who maintain "the old ways." But the biblical evidence for the church's claim to be the people of God points in another direction. All the New Testament authors were conscious of their Jewish spiritual roots, and Paul was convinced that there was still a place for unbelieving Israel within God's plan of salvation. Furthermore, attention to the particular historical settings of the Gospels of Matthew and John shows that the most blatant "anti-

---

[6]K. Stendahl, *Paul Among Jews and Gentiles and Other Essays* (Philadelphia: Fortress Press, 1976).

[7]S. Sandmel, *Anti-Semitism in the New Testament?* (Philadelphia: Fortress Press, 1978). See also E. J. Fisher, *Faith without Prejudice: Rebuilding Christian Attitudes toward Judaism* (New York, Ramsey, and Toronto: Paulist Press, 1977).

Jewish" statements in the New Testament come from Jewish Christians speaking to predominantly Jewish-Christian churches engaged in a conflict with other Jews claiming to be God's people. To equate "the scribes and Pharisees" in Matthew and "the Jews" in John with all Jews of our time is anachronistic and ahistorical lunacy. That is not to deny that a great deal of such lunacy has taken place and still exists. But it seems to be more imperative than ever that pastors and church leaders today carry out their solemn obligation to teach God's people in Christ to read the Scriptures intelligently. When the statements about Jews in Matthew and John are read with no concern for their historical setting and original meaning, the church continues to encourage a very dark and dangerous facet of Western civilization.

The unbelief of Israel remained a mystery to Paul, and it remains such to the church today. But that is no justification for all the pathetic and barbarous attempts throughout the ages at rooting out Israel. These acts are only a source of shame to those who now claim to be God's people in Christ. Moreover, Paul reserved a place for "unbelieving Israel" within the economy of salvation and left it to God to bring his plan to its fulfillment. Of course, this should not prevent Christians from wanting to share their religious vision and fellowship with Jews today. To withhold from another what one perceives as a precious spiritual treasure is selfishness, and selfishness is never very admirable. But Paul's conviction that Israel has a place in God's plan also challenges Christian theologians today to think about the possibility of finding a positive significance in the continued existence of Judaism. To go on using Judaism as the "left hand" of Christian faith or even to be satisfied with including the Jews in Rahner's mass of "anonymous Christians" do not seem to be adequate responses. The positive significance of Judaism is a topic just beginning to surface in discussions between Christian theologians and their Jewish counterparts. For Christians, the question is this: What positive contribution to Christian faith today can be made by Judaism as an independent group that carries on the heritage of ancient Israel? It is too early to know what answers will come out of such discussions, but the question is surely an important one.

6. Unity within the people of God. In Christ the ethnic, social, and sexual differences between persons become relatively unimportant. So in Gal 3:28 Paul asserts: "There is neither Jew nor Greek, there is neither slave nor free, there is neither male nor female; for you are all one in Christ Jesus." The author of Ephesians picks up this theme in 2:14: "For he is our peace, who has made us both one, and has broken down the dividing wall of hostility." These texts do not say that the physical and social differences between people have ceased to exist entirely. The biblical writers were not that naive. But they do maintain that these distinctions are no longer terribly important. Frequently texts like Gal 3:28 and Eph 2:14 are used as slogans for radical social change or as justifications for social inertia. Rather, their more fundamental thrust is neither change nor inertia. Rather, their more fundamental thrust is to make us appreciate the awesome change that occurs in baptism and the attitudes that ought to prevail within the community of baptized Christians. Prescinding for the moment from those outside the Christian community, we Christians cannot afford to let ethnic, social, or sexual distinctions be the sole criteria for action or inaction within the church. Every baptized Christian has the same awesome dignity before God, and every baptized Christian as part of God's people deserves our highest respect. On the other hand, prejudices against other Christians and violence between Christians totally contradict the church's identity as God's people in Christ.[8]

7. The people's pilgrimage. The people of God is a pilgrim people seeking its way in the world and journeying toward

---

[8]W. Rader, *The Church and Racial Hostility: A History of Interpretation of Ephesians 2:11-22* (BGBE 20; Tübingen: Mohr-Siebeck, 1978).

rest with God. In Romans 9—11 Paul made an effort to discern the flow of God's plan for humanity and the church's place in it. He firmly believed that God was using the church composed of Jews and Gentiles for his own good and creative purposes. The author of Hebrews warned his community to avoid the lack of trust and the disobedience that characterized the Exodus generation's wandering in the wilderness. The history of the early churches is the story of minority groups finding their ways in a disinterested or even positively hostile environment. First Peter and Revelation illustrate that fact quite dramatically. The experiences of those churches that are captured in the foundational documents of the church should provide encouragement today not only for communities in places where Christians are few and the churches suffer organized persecution but also in places like America and western Europe where many of the church's cultural props are being removed and institutional change is proceeding at a dizzying pace. God's people in Christ is on a journey and cannot control everything that happens along the way. God himself is its guide and its goal, and fidelity to God is the only security available to God's people in Christ.

9. SOCIOLOGICAL CONCEPTS AND THE EARLY CHURCH: A DECADE OF RESEARCH

During the past ten years the biblical-theological study of the church seems to have stood still. Of course, there have been good presentations of the topics that constitute the agenda of this approach: the relation between Jesus and the church, the images of the church, diversity of structures, and forms of ministry. Nevertheless, the positions taken and the methods that underlie them are not substantially different from the ones in fashion in the 1960's. Perhaps we should simply be satisfied with the solid results of the biblical-theological approach[1] and put our energies into making them more intelligible to nonspecialists. But there has been a development in biblical studies during the 1970's that may infuse some new life into the study of the church in the New Testament. It involves the use of the concepts and methods of sociology.

In North America to a great extent and in Europe to a lesser degree the social sciences are playing an increasing role in academic life. Many of the problems and concerns

---

[1] H. Küng, *The Church* (London: Burns and Oates, 1967; Garden City, NY: Image, 1976), is a well written and intelligible example of this approach.

traditionally treated in philosophy have been taken over by psychology, anthropology, and sociology. Even in the traditionally philological disciplines like orientalism[2] and biblical studies,[3] the influx of the social sciences has been noticeable. Those whose primary academic training is in the social sciences now apply their concepts and methods to fields in which philology had reigned.

The past decade has seen the introduction of sociological concepts to the study of the church in the NT, and this article gathers together that research and explores what impact it might have for our understanding of the early church and even of the church today. The presentation is restricted to those books and articles that make explicit use of sociological ideas and methods. It does not treat developments in the social description of early Christianity[4] or studies of individual documents in the NT, though in the long run such investigations will probably be recognized as more important than the material treated here.

What does the sociological approach do? Gerd Theissen[5] has defined the sociology of early Christianity as the description and analysis of typical, interpersonal behavior displayed by members of early Christian groups. It pays special attention to extraordinary events and conflicts, explicit and implicit norms of conduct, the use of symbols, innovations, causes of success or failure, and adjustments from charismatic to institutional forces. It illumines NT texts by analogies drawn from other religious movements. When comparing the early church with religious move-

[2] E. Said, *Orientalism* (New York: Pantheon, 1978).

[3] S. Brown, "Biblical Philology, Linguistics and the Problem of Method," *HeyJ* 20 (1979) 295-98.

[4] J. G. Gager in *RelSRev* 5 (1979) 174-80 has drawn attention to the important distinction between the social descriptions presented by R. M. Grant, A. J. Malherbe, and others, and the thoroughgoing use of sociological methods by G. Theissen.

[5] "Die soziologische Auswertung religioser Uberlieferungen. Ihre methodologischen Probleme am Beispiel des Urchristentums," *Kairos* 17 (1975) 284-99.

ments from the same time and place (e.g., the Essenes, the Pharisees), it focuses on points of contrast. When the movements differ radically in date and cultural setting, the constants are stressed.

The sociological approach calls on concepts that have proved successful in the sociology of religion.[6] Among these concepts are anomie, the charismatic prophet, the disprivileged, the routinization of charisma, collective emotion, legitimation, cosmization, and elective affinity. It tries to explain the meaning of words and ideas in relation to the historical situations and cultural contexts of the persons who used them.[7] The approach corresponds to a large extent to what in biblical studies has been termed the "setting in life" or *Sitz im Leben*. According to K. Berger,[8] this approach can lead exegetes toward the "location" of the documents (place, time, group, tradition-historical background), the roles of groups and of carriers of traditions, the christological "life center" operative in the early Christian adaptation of traditions, the process by which opposing groups and positions were brought into harmony, the relation between ideology and activity, and the extent to which theological statements are historically conditioned.

The obstacles to using sociological techniques in NT studies are formidable. They are obvious even to the most ardent proponents of the approach.[9] There is the obstacle posed by the historical distance of some nineteen hundred years. There is no way to use the refined techniques of

[6]E. Stevenson, "Some Insights from the Sociology of Religion into the Origin and Development of the Early Christian Church," *ExpT* 90 (1979) 300-305.

[7]D. Nineham, "A Partner for Cinderella?" *What About the New Testament? Essays in Honour of Christopher Evans* (ed. M. Hooker and C. Hickling; London: SCM, 1975) 143-54. See also Nineham's *The Use and Abuse of the Bible. A study of the Bible in an age of rapid cultural change* (Library of Philosophy and Religion; New York: Barnes & Noble/Harper & Row, 1977).

[8]"Wissenssoziologie und Exegese des Neuen Testaments," *Kairos* 19 (1977) 124-33. See also his *Exegese des Neuen Testaments. Neue Wege vom Text zur Auslegung* (Uni-Taschenbücher 658; Heidelberg: Quelle & Meyer, 1977).

[9]G. Theissen, "Theoretische Probleme religionssoziologischer Forschung und die Analyse des Urchristentums," *Neue Zeitschrift für systematische Theologie und Religionsphilosophie* 16 (1974) 35-56.

observation on the early church that one might use on a cult today. Furthermore, the NT writings are religious documents, and sociology has no satisfactory method for dealing with the divine or nonrational element that is so important in religious experience. Finally, the concepts and models of sociology are not absolutes. They represent conclusions drawn from the careful observation of particular movements or groups. They are subject to the tests and verification processes of the scientific method; they are not necessarily built into the structure of creation.

Given the reality of these obstacles, what can one hope to gain from the sociological approach to the development of the early church as witnessed in the NT? As I have mentioned, the biblical-theological approach has been fruitful but now seems to need a new lease on life. Perhaps the importing of new ideas and new concepts from the most obviously relevant of the social sciences will exercise a salutary effect, at least to the extent of making biblical theologians more conscious of their own concerns and methods. Moreover, it is possible that the sociological approach will make more intelligible the data presented in the NT and render less foreign the experiences of the people described in those documents. The decision as to whether this approach is of value depends entirely on whether it sheds light on the texts. There is at least the antecedent probability that this will be the case. Lastly, the approach should contribute to the dialogue between theologians and social scientists by providing new questions for both parties to ponder.

Two Major Contributions

The two most extensive attempts at applying the concepts of sociology to the development of the early church have been carried out by John G. Gager and Gerd Theissen. Gager[10] explores the relevance of conceiving Christianity as

[10]*Kingdom and Community. The Social World of Early Christianity* (Studies in Religion; Englewood Cliffs, NJ: Prentice-Hall, 1975).

a social world in the making with reference to the following issues: the relationship between religion and social status, the enthusiastic character of the earliest Christian communities, their gradual transformation into a formidable religious and social institution, and the emergence of Christianity as the dominant religion of the later Roman empire. The approach is theoretical and comparative: theoretical in the sense that explanatory models drawn from the social sciences are used, and comparative in that much of the evidence for these models is based on studies of non-Christian religious movements.

In the course of his presentation, Gager calls on certain terms and ideas developed in the sociology of religion as a help toward understanding the development of the early church. For example, the group gathered around Jesus is classed as a millenarian movement. Such groups believe that the present order will soon be overthrown or reversed, and that the promise of a heaven on earth will be fulfilled. They draw heavily from the disprivileged, from those who are either economically poor or perceive themselves to be shut out of the centers of power. In millenarian movements the charismatic prophet plays the part of a catalyst in articulating the complaints of the disprivileged and in symbolizing the contours of the new humanity. According to Gager, Jesus was a charismatic prophet for a millenarian movement. Even when Jesus' death and the delay of the kingdom seemed to disconfirm the movement's hopes, the group did not die. Instead, it threw itself into a vigorous round of missionary activity.[11]

Perhaps more significant than the church's origin as a millenarian movement was its development into a sociologi-

---

[11]For discussions of cognitive dissonance in early Christianity, see H. Jackson, "The Resurrection Belief of the Earliest Church: A Response to the Failure of Prophecy?" *JR* 55 (1975) 415-25; and U. Wernik, "Frustrated beliefs and early Christianity. A Psychological Enquiry into the Gospels of the New Testament," *Numen* 22 (1975) 96-130. For social-science treatments of the traditions about Jesus, see E. L. Abel, "The Psychology of Memory and Rumor Transmission and Their Bearing on Theories of Oral Transmission in Early Christianity," *JR* 51 (1971) 270-81; and R. B. Williams, "Reflections on the Transmission of Tradition in the Early Church," *Encounter* 40 (1979) 273-85.

cally viable and distinguishable (from Judaism) institution. Here Gager calls on Max Weber's idea of the routinization of charisma. Far from being limited to the initial stages of enthusiastic movements, charisma is viewed as a fundamental component of all institutions at every stage of their existence: "Charismatic authority and the rise of institutional structures are complementary, not antithetical movements" (87). For the first two hundred years of its existence Christianity was essentially a movement among the disprivileged (economically or socially) within the Roman empire. It incorporated the characteristics of the religion of the disprivileged: a strong tendency toward congregational units, a reliance on future-oriented compensation (salvation), and a rational system of ethics. Why did Christianity succeed? The existence of Hellenistic Judaism in the Diaspora and the peaceful conditions in the Roman empire were the most powerful external factors. The most prominent internal factor was the radical sense of community—open to all, insistent on absolute and exclusive loyalty, and concerned with every aspect of the believer's life.

Three critical articles in *Zygon* have called attention to the problems involved in Gager's approach. D. L. Bartlett[12] observed that Gager's book is interesting and important more because of what it attempts than what it accomplishes. Questions are raised about the use of sociological models to provide new data, the unclear categories and the uncertain force of the argument, the tendency to homogenize the evidence about early Christianity, the disparity between the evidence and some of the theories, and the lack of attention to the peculiarly religious aspects of early Christianity. According to J. Z. Smith,[13] Gager refuses to accept historical particularities and their consequences, to take seriously the context of the sociological and anthropological models he employs, and to engage in serious methodological and theoretical meditation on the issues raised by them. D.

[12]"John G. Gager's 'Kingdom and Community': A Summary and Response," *Zygon* 13 (1978) 109-22.
[13]"Too Much Kingdom, Too Little Community," *Zygon* 13 (1978) 123-30.

Tracy[14] pleads for the inclusion of fundamental theology in the dialogue between social scientists and historians of religion and for more attention to the internal factor operative in early Christianity.

Gerd Theissen's sociology of early Palestinian Christianity between A.D. 30 and 70 is less ambitious.[15] After defining his task as the description of typical social attitudes and behavior within the Jesus movement and the analysis of its interactions with Jewish society in Palestine, he discusses the wandering charismatics[16] and their sympathizers based in local communities, and then interprets the Son of Man Christology as expressing the experience of the wandering charismatics. In treating the influences of the broader society on the Jesus movement, he examines various factors: socioeconomic (rootlessness),[17] socioecological (rural ambivalence toward Jerusalem),[18] sociopolitical (nominal theocracy versus the *de facto* aristocracy), and sociocultural (intensification of norms as a reaction toward assimilation). The final section of the book deals with the Jesus movement's functions in containing aggression and its relative lack of success in Palestine.

---

[14]"A Theological Response to 'Kingdom and Community,' " *Zygon* 13 (1978) 131-35.

[15]*Soziologie der Jesusbewegung. Ein Beitrag zur Entstehungsgeschichte des Urchristentums* (Theologische Existenz heute 194; Munich: Kaiser, 1977). The American edition is *Sociology of Early Palestinian Christianity* (Philadelphia: Fortress, 1978) and the British edition is *The First Followers of Jesus* (London: SCM, 1978).

[16]"Wanderradikalismus. Literatursoziologische Aspekte der Überlieferung von Worten Jesu im Urchristentum," *ZTK* 70 (1973) 245-71. See also "Legitimation und Lebensunterhalt: Ein Beitrag zur Soziologie urchristlicher Missionare," *NTS* 21 (1974-75) 192-221.

[17]" 'Wir haben alles verlassen' (MC. X 28). Nachfolge und soziale Entwurzelung in der jüdisch-palästinischen Gesellschaft des I. Jahrhunderts n. Ch.," *NovT* 19 (1977) 161-96.

[18]"Die Tempelweissagung Jesu. Prophetie im Spannungsfeld von Stadt und Land," *TZ* 32 (1976) 144-58. See also H. G. Kippenberg, *Religion und Klassenbildung im antiken judäa. Eine religionssoziologische Studie zum Verhältnis von Tradition und gesellschaftlicher Entwicklung* (WUNT 14; Göttingen: Vandenhoeck & Ruprecht, 1978).

Theissen's sociological base is functional analysis.[19] He relies heavily on conflict analysis; he assumes that religious renewal movements develop out of social tensions and attempt to give new impulses for their resolution. In addition to leaving himself open to some of the general criticisms raised in the first part of this report and to some of the points made against Gager's book, Theissen appears at times to force the data to fit his theories. For example, the poverty and social uprootedness of the Galilean fishermen among Jesus' disciples (34) are strongly emphasized, even though in a preindustrial economy fishermen exercised a relatively secure and profitable trade. Also, apocalypticism is interpreted in a somewhat simple manner as a protest against economic and social conditions. But apocalyptic movements arise in a variety of social conditions, even among college-educated men and women of the United States in the 1970's.

Other Contributions

The programmatic character of the books by Gager and Theissen should not obscure the fact that other NT scholars have been working in similar directions. B. J. Malina has explored some of the fundamental orientations or attitudes that structured the experiences and expressions of people in the Greco-Roman world of the first century A.D. He has drawn attention to the image of the limited good; that is, all the desired things in life exist in finite quantity and are always in short supply.[20] This image can be glimpsed in the understanding of the ideal person as one who neither encroaches on others nor allows himself to be exploited, the discovery of success or wealth at the interfaces of one's closed system or social station, and the search for patrons within the cosmos (God, Satan, angels or spirits, etc.).

[19]J. G. Gager, *RelSRev* 5 (1979) 174-80.
[20]"Limited Good and the Social World of Early Christianity," *BTB* 8 (1978) 162-76.

Malina has also investigated the importance of "dyadic personality" in the Mediterranean world of the Hellenistic period.[21] The term "dyadic personality" describes individuals as embedded within the group and their behavior as determined by significant others.

The dynamics of millenarian movements with reference to early Christianity have been explored by S. R. Isenberg. In Greco-Roman Palestine the issue that divided the various groups was access to and/or control over the redemptive media, especially the temple cult and the Law.[22] Members of millenarian movements like the Essenes and the Christians felt blocked off from the redemptive media. These movements developed according to the following pattern: (1) the feeling of deprivation and oppression, (2) the concrete expresssion and testing of the new assumptions and beliefs about power along with the appearance of a millenarian prophet, and (3) consolidation or dissolution. Within this framework Isenberg situates the Qumran Teacher of Righteousness, Jesus, and Paul as millenarian prophets.[23] All three claimed authority outside the normal channels of power in the Jewish community, relied on access to a higher truth and a higher power in direct revelation, and drew followings responsive to the messages of hope for the deprived.

Gershom Scholem's massive study of Sabbatai Sevi, a Jewish messianic figure from the seventeenth century A.D.,[24] has been hailed by sociologist Daniel Bell not only as a work of magisterial historical scholarship but also as "the most subtle and complex exploration I know of the character of messianic movements and messianic longings ... "[25]

---

[21]"The Individual and the Community—Personality in the SocialWorld of Early Christianity," *BTB* 9 (1979) 126-38. See also G. S. Worgul, "Anthropological Consciousness and Biblical Theology," *BTB* 9 (1979) 3-12.

[22]"Millenarism in Greco-Roman Palestine," *Religion* 4 (1974) 26-46.

[23]"Power through Temple and Torah in Greco-Roman Palestine," *Christianity, Judaism and Other Greco-Roman Cults. Studies for Morton Smith at Sixty. Part 2: Early Christianity* (ed. J. Neusner; SJLA 12; Leiden: Brill, 1975) 24-52.

[24]*Sabbatai Ṣevi. The Mystical Messiah 1626-1676* (Bollingen Series 93; Princeton, NJ: Princeton University, 1973).

[25]"Immortal Nominations," *New York Times Book Review* (3 June 1979) 12.

The parallels between that seventeenth-century Jewish movement and early Christianity have been explored by W. D. Davies.[26] The primary phenomena of a messianic movement are said to be the radical confrontation with the established order so that faith in the messiah becomes crucial, and the ability to convey the living experience of redemption to many people in many places. Among the secondary characteristics are religious enthusiasm, miracles, the nature and activity of the messiah (hidden, suffering, not having an army, etc.), overcoming death, significant interpreters, and relatively little interest in the messiah's history and character. For all their similarities, Christianity and Sabbatianism are said to differ in two important aspects: (1) the conceptual background of early Christianity was far more complex and varied; (2) the constructive constraint of Jesus' ministry stands in marked contrast to the negative, distorting, and ultimately nihilistic influence of Sabbatai.

These discussions of early Christianity as a millenarian movement naturally lead to analyses of it as a sect. According to R. Scroggs,[27] the community called into existence by Jesus fulfills the essential characteristics of the religious sect as defined in recent sociological investigation. It emerged out of protest, rejected the reality claimed by the establishment, was egalitarian in its communal life, offered acceptance and love within the community, was a voluntary association, demanded total commitment from its members, and had an apocalyptic or adventist perspective. W. A. Meeks[28] has drawn attention to the fundamental ambiguity in the social character of the Pauline churches. On the one hand, the church was an eschatological sect with

[26]"From Schweitzer to Scholem: Reflections on Sabbatai Svi," *JBL* 95 (1976) 529-58.

[27]"The Earliest Christian Communities as Sectarian Movement," *Christianity, Judaism and Other Greco-Roman Cults. Studies for Morton Smith at Sixty. Part 2: Early Christianity* (ed. J. Neusner; SJLA 12; Leiden: Brill, 1975) 1-23.

[28] 'Since Then You Would Need To Go Out Of The World': Group Boundaries in Pauline Christianity," *Critical History and Biblical Faith* (ed. T. J. Ryan; Villanova, PA: College Theology Society/ Horizons, 1979) 4-29.

a strong sense of group boundaries. On the other hand, it was an open sect, concerned not to offend outsiders but to attract them to its message and membership. This was an inherently unstable combination, though an enormously creative one. The boundaries between the Pauline churches and the society around them were defined by special language emphasizing separation (the chosen, brothers and sisters, the saints, etc.), rules, the penalty of exclusion from common meals, the creation of autonomous institutions to serve the members, and sanctioned interactions with the society at large.

The Christian community at Corinth has been the subject of several sociological studies. In a fascinating series of articles, Theissen has focused on the social classes that made up that church. The references to official positions, households, provisions made for missionaries and for the community, and journeys to distant places in connection with many of the Corinthians mentioned by name in the NT indicate that the upper classes constituted a substantial part of that group, though not the majority (see 1 Cor 1:26).[29] In fact, the "strong" and the "weak" may correlate with the different social levels in the Corinthian community. This class differentiation was probably the background of the controversy over eating meat sacrificed to idols (see 1 Cor 8)[30] and the conflict over the common meal (see 1 Cor 11:17-34).[31] The Christian community at Corinth has also been studied by A. Schreiber,[32] who relies heavily on theories of group process and group dynamics from the social sciences. He deals with the formation of the community into

[29]"Soziale Schichtung in der korinthischen Gemeinde. Ein Beitrag zur Soziologie des hellenistischen Urchristentums," *ZNW* 65 (1974) 232-72.

[30]"Die Starken und Schwachen in Korinth. Soziologische Analyse eines theologischen Streites," *EvT* 35 (1975) 155-72.

[31]"Soziale Integration und sakramentales Handeln. Eine Analyse von I Cor. XI 17-34," *NovT* 16 (1974) 179-206.

[32]*Die Gemeinde in Korinth. Versuch einer gruppendynamischen Betrachtung der Entwicklung der Gemeinde von Korinth auf der Basis der ersten Korintherbriefes* (NTAbh 12; Münster: Aschendorff, 1977). See the perceptive review by J. H. Elliott in *Bib* 59 (1978) 589-92.

a group, its functioning as a group (interactions, group feeling, norms, goals and roles, direction and leadership, etc.), Paul's departure from Corinth and the activity of Apollos, and the exchange of letters between Paul and the Corinthian community. Schreiber is also concerned with the methodological implications of applying social-science techniques to the New Testament and with the light they can shed on the development of primitive Christian communities.

Another important sociological contribution to Pauline studies has been made by J. H. Schütz's work on charisma and social reality.[33] According to him, Paul viewed charisma as ordering the common life by establishing priorities and discriminating among competing manifestations of the Spirit. It also ordered the individual life by providing the coordinates of its locus within a common framework. If one proceeds on Max Weber's view that charisma is self-determined and sets its own limits, then Paul could not be counted as a charismatic. Weber's scheme fits Paul's opponents better than it fits Paul. Rather, Paul's understanding of charisma is closer to that of Edward Shils, who maintains that the phenomenon of charismatic authority is not inimical to organizational structure.

Implications for Exegesis and Theology

This report has gathered together some of the most important books and articles published in the 1970's that explicitly use sociological concepts for understanding the origin and development of the church in the NT. I have freely admitted the limitations of the sociological approach: the historical gulf, the nontheological orientation of sociology, and the questionable validity of some sociological models. Nevertheless, the sociological study of the NT

---

[33]"Charisma and Social Reality in Primitive Christianity," *JR* 54 (1974) 51-70. See also his *Paul and the Anatomy of Apostolic Authority* (SNTSMS 26; New York: Cambridge University, 1975).

church begun during the past decade promises to make an even greater impact during the 1980's and so we should try to sketch what contributions we can expect it to make to exegesis and theology.[34]

The least that we can expect from the sociological approach is a set of new questions, terms, and analogies for studying the church in the NT period. For example, anyone who has studied the Sabbatian movement in seventeenth-century Judaism is bound to return to the Jesus movement of the first century with new perspectives on Jesus' free attitude toward the Law, the roles of John the Baptist and Paul in the movement, the reactions to Jesus' death, and the reinterpretation of the Scriptures in the light of Jesus. Familiarity with the Sabbatian movement should make us more cautious about declaring "unthinkable" some of the things attributed to the earthly Jesus in the Gospels. Furthermore, the sociological approach uses the vocabulary and methodology gaining increasing prominence in the study of religion. This is not to say that the concerns and vocabulary of theology should be abandoned. But theologians ought to be willing and able to join in conversation with researchers who investigate religious phenomena from other perspectives. Finally, the use of sociological analogies and concepts can provide exegetes with clues and hypotheses about the communal setting of NT documents. The great interpreters from Origen to Bultmann have studied biblical texts with an eye toward individual experience and have relied on various kinds of philosophical anthropology. Yet critics of this personalist approach always point to the communal and social character of the NT writings. They correctly demand a hermeneutic more appropriate to the material being studied. Perhaps the critical use of sociological concepts will help toward developing a socially-oriented method of interpretation.

---

[34]In my monograph *God's People in Christ: New Testament Perspectives on the Church and Judaism* (Overtures to Biblical Theology; Philadelphia: Fortress, 1980), I use some sociological concepts in a biblical-theological investigation of the church as the people of God.

The most that we can expect from the sociological approach is that it will exercise a significant and even revolutionary effect on the application of the historical-critical method. During the 1970's the sociological approach has been very general in its statements; there was a need to get the ideas and terms into the mainstream of the discussion. The material reviewed in this article is only a beginning and needs to be surpassed by more detailed analyses of individual texts. The value of the sociological approach will be proved primarily by its ability to illumine obscure texts and to provide insight into the social situations in which Christianity arose and developed. The emergence of this new approach in the 1970's means that exegetes and theologians of the 1980's have some new items on their agenda. They must be more sensitive to clues concerning the economic, social, and cultural levels of the people mentioned in the NT documents (writers, addressees, opponents, etc.). They must try to determine more precisely the nature of the social conflicts underlying the texts and to discern the principles and methods by which those conflicts were resolved. They must pay more attention to better-documented religious phenomena from other times and other cultures, and explore more critically what value this or that sociological concept might have for understanding aspects of the origin and development of the church in the New Testament.

10. THE RECEPTION OF WALTER BAUER'S *ORTHODOXY AND HERESY IN EARLIEST CHRISTIANITY* DURING THE LAST DECADE

First published in 1934, Walter Bauer's *Rechtgläubigkeit und Ketzerei im ältesten Christentum*[1] warned against simply equating the words "orthodoxy" and "heresy" with the notions of majority and minority and with the process of deviation from correct belief to wrong belief. Bauer sought to show that in the first two Christian centuries orthodoxy and heresy did not stand in relation to one another as primary and secondary. He tried to prove that in many regions what came to be known in the ecclesiastical tradition as "heresy" was in fact the original manifestation of Christianity. For example, according to Bauer, the major figures in earliest Christianity at Edessa were the "heretics" Marcion, Bar Daisan, and Mani. In Egypt a gnostic form of Christianity appears to have been dominant before A.D. 200, and in Asia Minor "orthodox" leaders such as Ignatius and Polycarp waged only moderately successful battles against gnosticism and judaizing Christianity.

In Bauer's reconstruction of early Christian history, orthodoxy or ecclesiastical Christianity represented the

---

[1] It appeared as volume 10 in the series BHTh= Beiträge zur historischen Theologie (Tübingen: Mohr-Siebeck, 1934).

type supported by the majority of Christians in Rome at the end of the first century and the beginning of the second century. The Roman church then gradually extended the boundaries of its influence to Corinth (see *1 Clement*), Antioch, and other places. It did so through its traditional associations with Peter and Paul, its successful interventions in the affairs of other churches, timely financial donations, compassionate attitude toward repentant sinners, and effective leadership and tight organization under a single bishop. Orthodox and heretical groups used similar tactics; e.g., repeating false rumors, not recognizing false believers as fellow believers, not admitting anything good about opponents, emphasizing their weaknesses and inadequacies, and supporting or even falsifying their views. But in the course of the early Christian centuries the so-called heretical groups remained divided and even fought among themselves. They were finally routed, one after another, by so-called orthodox Christians.

Because of the political conditions prevailing in Germany during the late 1930s and the very technical style in which the book was written, the German original did not receive the attention that it deserved. After 1934 Bauer turned from church history and devoted his energies to preparing his monumental Greek lexicon of the NT and other early Christian writings. But the corrections and annotations entered prior to his death in 1960 in his personal copy of the original publication were included in George Strecker's 1964 edition. Strecker also provided an appendix on the problem of Jewish Christianity and a survey of reactions to Bauer's thesis in general. In 1971 the English translation made by members of the Philadelphia Seminar on Christian Origins was published under the general editorship of Robert A. Kraft and Gerhard Krodel.[2] In the English version Strecker's discussion of the reception of the book was revised and expanded by Kraft, and the resulting appendix

---

[2]*Orthodoxy and Heresy in Earliest Christianity* (Philadelphia: Fortress, 1971). The British edition was published by SCM of London in 1972.

published on pp. 286-316 constitutes a valuable feature of the English edition. This brief article aims to bring up to date Strecker's and Kraft's appendix on the book's reception by reporting on reviews of the English translation, articles that criticize aspects of Bauer's thesis and a doctoral dissertation analyzing the theory as a whole, and two important books that develop Bauer's thesis in positive directions.

Reviews

The following list supplies data on the reviews of *Orthodoxy and Heresy in Earliest Christianity* that were published in North American periodicals: E. Earle Ellis, *Reformed Review* 27 (1973) 22-23; Daniel J. Harrington, *America* 125 (1971) 75; George Johnston, *Studies in Religion/Sciences Religieuses* 2 (1972-73) 365-66; A. Thomas Kraabel, *Encounter* 33 (1972) 416-18; Richard N. Longenecker, *Christianity Today* 16 (1971-72) 663-64; Lynn A. McMillon, *Journal of Church and State* 14 (1972) 142-44; Cecilia Murphy, *Review for Religious* 31 (1972) 151-52; Maurice Schild, *Lutheran World* 19 (1972) 302; Bruce Vawter, *CBQ* 34 (1972) 201-2; and Paul Woolley, *WTJ* 34 (1971-72) 183-86. The judgment that appears most frequently in the North American reviews is "provocative" (Harrington, Johnston, Kraabel, McMillon)—an appreciative though cautious term. Yet even those who are the most critical of Bauer's general approach call the book influential (Ellis) and "epochal" (Longenecker). The North American reviews repeat the old criticisms about Bauer's tendency to tailor the evidence to fit the thesis, his reliance on arguments from silence, his failure to define clearly the theology and practice of "orthodoxy," and his refusal to explore the theological significance of Roman Christianity's triumph. The most interesting comments in these reviews were made by Vawter and Kraabel. Vawter observed that Bauer's thesis about early Christian diversity did not seem as revolutionary in 1971 as it had in 1934, because it had been partly corroborated and partly paralleled by NT studies on the origins of

Christianity. Also noteworthy was Kraabel's suggestive comparison of Bauer's application of methods developed in the critical study of biblical documents to post-NT writings with an approach then emerging in the USA that "applies a variety of historical and social scientific methods to the ancient religion 'early Christianity' in its many forms, and attempts to understand and evaluate them all in the wider context of Greco-Roman piety" (p. 417).

The appearance of a British edition in 1972 prompted these reviews: W. H. C. Frend, *JTS* n.s. 24 (1973) 239; R. A. Markus, *New Blackfriars* 54 (1973) 283-84; John McHugh, *Clergy Review* 58 (1973) 237-39; G. C. Stead, *Theology* 76 (1973) 433-34; and Marcus Ward, *ExpT* 83 (1971-72) 313. British reactions to the appearance of Bauer's book were expressed in terms like "revolutionary" and "pioneering" (Frend), "seminal" (Markus, McHugh), "indisputably important" (Stead), and "brilliant and provocative" (Ward). Stead repeated with apparent agreement the criticisms previously raised about stretching the evidence to fit the thesis, relying on arguments from silence, and the odd understanding of orthodoxy. McHugh observed that, if Bauer's reconstruction is true, the traditional deposit of faith and the propositions about God and Jesus emerge as far less important than they have been taken in most Christian circles since the Council of Nicaea. The most intriguing comment came from Markus, who proposed that orthodoxy's confrontation with other sects in the second century ought to be seen as "a moment in a crystallizing self-awareness" instead of as an accident of ecclesiastical or political power.

Articles

Writing in 1977 on the 100th anniversary of Bauer's birth, George Strecker[3] observed that the basic aim of Bauer's

[3]"Walter Bauer—Exeget, Philologe und Historiker. Zum 100. Geburtstag am 8. 8. 1977," *NovT* 20 (1978) 75-80.

historical and philological research was to reveal the inherent weakness of all fundamentalist or biblicist presuppositions about the timeless character of the Bible. Several years previously, Jerry R. Flora[4] reviewed Bauer's achievements as lexicographer, exegete, and historian of the early church and gave special attention to his decision around 1934 to spend all his time on the lexicon of NT and other early Christian writings. But far more important and probing than the general reactions expressed in the North American and British reviews and these two biographical sketches were the many articles that took up specific features of Bauer's historical reconstruction and theological framework.

The applicability of Bauer's thesis to the NT was challenged on historical and methodological grounds. I. Howard Marshall[5] asserted that the only valid point in the thesis is that there was variety of belief in the first century but argued that Paul and the Evangelists combatted false teachings and that the distinction between orthodoxy and heresy already existed near the end of the first century. Writing with reference to the problem of the unity of the NT and not explicitly with regard to Bauer, Brice L. Martin[6] noted that the German discussion about unity and diversity is often marked by the reduction of all relationships to the harmonizable and the contradictory. This accounts for the assumption that the NT is filled with contradictions, and the large middle ground of diverse, noncomplementary, but compatible perspectives is left unnoticed.

Certain aspects of Bauer's reconstruction of early Christian history were also called into question. Recognizing that *1 Clement* is the key to Bauer's theory that the victory of orthodoxy was the victory of Roman authority over the churches, A. I. C. Heron[7] declared that Bauer's interpreta-

[4]"That Dictionary Man, Walter Bauer," *Ashland Theological Bulletin* 6 (1973) 3-11.

[5]"Orthodoxy and heresy in earlier Christianity," *Themelios* 2 (1976) 5-14.

[6]"Some reflections on the unity of the New Testament," *Studies in Religion/ Sciences Religieuses* 8 (1979) 143-52.

[7]"The Interpretation of I Clement in Walter Bauer's 'Rechtgläubigkeit und Ketzerei im ältesten Christentum,' " *Ekklesiastikos Pharos* 55 (1973) 517-45.

tion of that letter is inadequate on three counts: (1) The
analysis of Rome's motives as including the desire to extend
its influence depends more on late second-century evidence
than it does on *1 Clement*. (2) The description of the situation supposed to be prevailing at Corinth has no support in
the text. (3) The grounds for locating the writing of the letter
in the context of the struggle with heresy do not exist.
Bauer's interpretation of *1 Clement* is contradicted by so
many features in the text itself that Heron rejects it entirely.
The thrust of Heron's article is to suggest that the theory of
an original plurality of types of Christianity does not necessarily demand that Rome's operations should be assessed as
they are by Bauer.

According to R. van den Broek,[8] Bauer's view that Alexandrian Christianity before Clement of Alexandria was of a
predominantly gnostic character should now be corrected in
the light of three recently published Nag Hammadi trac-
tates: *Sentences of Sextus, Authoritative Teaching,* and
Teachings of Silvanus. These three documents were probably composed in Alexandria around the end of the second
century A.D., and their anthropology and soteriology suggest that in addition to the gnosticizing Christians at Alexandria there were also Christians strongly influenced by
Platonism.

Bauer's use of the term "heresy" was refined by Marcel
Simon,[9] who showed that early Christian writers used the
word *hairesis* in a variety of ways: for Jewish sects, Greek
philosophical schools, Christian sects. In pagan usage it
referred to a coherent and articulated doctrine founded on
principles of reason. The pagan antecedents for the Christian notion of heresy are to be found in the Greek concept of
heterodoxia ("the act of mistaking one thing for another").

In an effort to complement Bauer's thesis that unity was
not the original form of church life, Martin Elze[10] tried to

---

[8]"Niet-gnostisch Christendom in Alexandrië voor Clemens en Origenes,"
NedThTs 33 (1979) 287-99.

[9]"From Greek Hairesis to Christian Heresy," *Early Christian Literature and the
Classical Intellectual Tradition. In honorem Robert M. Grant* (ed. W.R. Schoedel
and R. L. Wilken; Théologie historique 54; Paris: Beauchesne, 1979) 101-16.

[10]"Häresie und Einheit der Kirche im 2. Jahrhundert," *ZTK* 71 (1974) 389-409.

show that from the beginnings of early Christianity unity was not conceived in doctrinal terms. Elze argued that church unity was related to unity of doctrine only in the second century and that the articulation of a Logos theology by the Christian apologists contributed to the shift in the application of the term *hairesis* from inner-church disharmony to differences in doctrine. But according to Adelbert Davids,[11] the classical theory of orthodoxy and heresy so vigorously challenged by Bauer was already present in the writings of Clement of Rome, Ignatius of Antioch, and Justin Martyr. Each of those early Christian writers appeared to be conscious of the temporal priority of the pure teaching delivered by Christ and the apostles that afterwards was corrupted by one or some few of the heretics.

Davids was not the only scholar who argued that "orthodoxy" was earlier and more widespread than Bauer allowed. In the opinion of Frederick W. Norris,[12] Bauer was unable to demonstrate that "heresy" was prior to and/or stronger than "orthodoxy" in Antioch and Asia Minor, could not establish that monepiscopacy did not exist there, and misunderstood the important distinctions between "heresy" and "orthodoxy" that appear in the literature and form the background for their later separation. The view that from the beginning of the second century the Roman community was singularly the dominant force in the formation of orthodoxy is rejected by Norris. According to James F. McCue,[13] Bauer overlooked certain aspects of Valentinian thought that told seriously against his thesis that Valentinianism was a form of Christianity independent of orthodoxy in its origins. Examination of references to Valentinianism made by Irenaeus, Clement of Alexandria, and Heracleon led McCue to draw these conclusions: (1) The orthodox play a role in Valentinian thought such that

[11]"Irrtum und Häresie. 1 Clem.—Ignatius von Antiochien—Justinus," *Kairos* 15 (1973) 165-87.

[12]"Ignatius, Polycarp, and I Clement: Walter Bauer Reconsidered," *VC* 30 (1976) 23-44.

[13]"Orthodoxy and Heresy: Walter Bauer and the Valentinians," *VC* 33 (1979) 118-30.

they seem to be part of Valentinian self-understanding. (2) The orthodox appear to be the main body and at several points are identified as the many over against the small number of Valentinians. (3) The Valentinians of the decades prior to Irenaeus and Clement of Alexandria used the books of the orthodox NT in a manner best accounted for by supposing that Valentinianism developed within a mid-second-century orthodox matrix.

Articles by G. Clarke Chapman, Jr. and David J. Hawkin investigated the theological problems raised by Bauer's work. Chapman[14] suggested that, if the historical and sociological reconstruction proposed by Bauer should prove to be correct, perhaps "orthodoxy" should be assessed as the most accurate and adequate theological interpretation of the Christ-event and the possibility should be raised that God's mysterious grace was at work through the institution of the church at Rome. Hawkin[15] criticized Bauer for failing to settle on a heuristic definition of orthodoxy and judged Henry E. W. Turner's[16] hermeneutical starting point (the *lex orandi* and the dynamic unity of Christian development) to be more faithful to the Christian conviction that the selfhood of Christianity was born "from above" and guided by God.

The most extensive critical analysis of Bauer's theory of early Christian orthodoxy and heresy was the 1972 doctoral dissertation (unpublished) by Jerry R. Flora.[17] After situating Bauer's theory in the context of his career, Flora examined its roots in German Protestant historiography of early Christianity, evaluated Bauer's thesis as a historical expla-

[14]"Some Theological Reflections on Walter Bauer's *Rechtgläubigkeit und Ketzerei im ältesten Christentum:* A Review Article," *JES* 7 (1970) 564-74.

[15]"A Reflective Look at the Recent Debate on Orthodoxy and Heresy in Earliest Christianity," *Eglise et théologie* 7 (1976) 367-78.

[16]*The Pattern of Christian Truth: A Study in the Relations Between Orthodoxy and Heresy in the Early Church* (London: Mowbray, 1954).

[17]"A Critical Analysis of Walter Bauer's Theory of Early Christian Orthodoxy and Heresy," directed by Harold O. Songer and accepted by Southern Baptist Theological Seminary in 1972. A summary appears in *Dissertation Abstracts* 33 (1973) 5276-A.

nation, and described the various scholarly reactions to it. Flora called Bauer's theory "a brilliant, but one-sided, corrective to the traditional view put forward by the early heresiologists," but added that there are good reasons for tempering each point in Bauer's outline. According to Flora, what emerged as orthodoxy around A.D. 200 was the church's best choice in the circumstances and exhibited both historical continuity and theological balance.

Books

Since Bauer touched on almost every aspect of early Christian history and since his book has been influential in scholarly circles during the past forty-five years, practically any contribution to NT and patristic scholarship can be viewed as a development of his theory. But two books—one a study of the NT and the other a treatment of the gnostic Gospels—stand out as explicit and powerful developments of Bauer's views. The fact that these two books rank among the most important studies of early Christianity published during the 1970's indicates the continuing significance of Bauer's pioneering research.

In his magnificent investigation of unity and diversity in the NT, James D. G. Dunn[18] takes as one of his purposes the task of exploring the issues raised by Bauer with reference to the NT. Of course Helmut Koester[19] had already refined and extended Bauer's historical schema back into the "apostolic age," and the fact of the diversity of theological viewpoints

---

[18]*Unity and Diversity in the New Testament. An Inquiry Into the Character of Earliest Christianity* (Philadelphia: Westminster, 1977). This is a sequel to Dunn's *Jesus and the Spirit. A Study of the Religious and Charismatic Experience of Jesus and the First Christians as Reflected in the New Testament* (Philadelphia: Westminster, 1975).

[19]"*GNŌMAI DIAPHOROI*: The Origin and Nature of Diversification in the History of Early Christianity," *HTR* 58 (1965) 279-318; reprinted in James M. Robinson and Helmut Koester, *Trajectories through Early Christianity* (Philadelphia: Fortress, 1971) 114-57. In the epilogue to *Trajectories,* Koester wrote: "Walter Bauer was right when he singled out particular regions for his description of orthodoxy and heresy (p. 273)." The significance of Koester's article was discussed by Strecker and Kraft in pp. 309-10 of the English translation.

within the NT has become a commonplace. Nevertheless, no one had tested the validity of applying Bauer's thesis to NT theology and history on such a grand scale as Dunn now has. After remarks on whether "orthodoxy" is a meaningful concept in the NT period, Dunn discussed early Christian preaching, primitive confessional formulas, the role of tradition, the use of the OT, concepts of ministry, patterns of worship, sacraments, spirit and experience, and Christ and Christology. The second part of Dunn's book maps out the diversity among early Christian groups under these headings: Jewish Christianity, Hellenistic Christianity, apocalyptic Christianity, and early catholicism. Dunn concludes that (1) the unifying strand marking out Christianity as something distinctive and providing the integrating center for the diverse expressions of Christianity was the unity between the historical Jesus and the exalted Christ, and (2) the expression of this unifying strand is radically diverse— so diverse that one must admit that there was no single normative form of Christianity in the first century.

A second important development of Bauer's thesis is Elaine Pagels' investigation of the gnostic Gospels.[20] Written for a general audience and extraordinarily well publicized, this book represents both a resurrection of Bauer's thesis and a development of it on the basis of the discovery of the Nag Hammadi documents and research on them since 1945. Pagels compares the treatments of six major topics in the gnostic Gospels with what came to be accepted as the orthodox position. The six topics are the resurrection of Christ as historical event or as symbol, the politics of monotheism and its implications for church structure, God as father and mother, the passion of Christ and the persecution of Christians, the true church and membership in it, and self-knowledge as knowledge of God. Faithful to Bauer's basic insight, Pagels sees the gnostic and the orthodox forms of Christianity as variant interpretations of the teaching and significance of Christ.

[20] *The Gnostic Gospels* (New York: Random House, 1979).

Conclusion

That so many NT and patristic scholars are still interested in Walter Bauer's *Rechtgläubigkeit und Ketzerei im ältesten Christentum* nearly fifty years after its initial publication is ample testimony to its importance. During the early 1970's the English translation was widely reviewed, and throughout the decade there appeared articles taking issue with this or that point in Bauer's historical reconstruction or theological outlook. Two major books on early Christianity used Bauer's thesis as their starting point. All this attention for a book almost a half-century old!

Where does Bauer's thesis about orthodoxy and heresy stand as we move into the 1980's? Obviously much of the historical analysis has to be redone and refined in the light of recent textual and archaeological discoveries (Koester, Pagels, van den Broek). But if we confine ourselves to what is presented in Bauer's book, it seems that discussion during the 1970's has drawn attention to some fundamental problems. The thesis of early Christian diversity is well established (Dunn, Marshall), but Bauer's reconstruction of how orthodoxy triumphed remains questionable. And one does not have to defend the Eusebian or "classical" reconstruction of early Christian history in order to reject Bauer's. On the historical level it is important to recognize that there is no necessary connection between Bauer's discovery of diversity everywhere in earliest Christianity and the historical reconstruction of how the Roman church imposed its brand of orthodoxy on the other churches (Heron).[21]

With regard to methodology Bauer's book still makes fascinating reading even fifty years after its original appearance. Everywhere there is philological mastery, admirable control of sources, and evidence of a sharp and penetrating intellect. But the lack of interest in Greco-Roman history

[21] The same point is made by H. J. W. Drijvers in "Rechtgläubigkeit und Ketzerei im ältesten syrischen Christentum," *Symposium Syriacum 1972* (Orientalia Christiana Analecta 197; Rome: Pontificum Institutum Orientalium Studiorum, 1974) 291-310.

and social scientific theory is striking (Kraabel). Since Bauer was mainly concerned with the interactions between early Christian groups, the failure to invoke the researches of Max Weber and other sociologists as complements to his literary analysis is surprising. At any rate, those who intend to follow in Bauer's footsteps must pay more attention to the basic concepts of sociology in working out the relations between "orthodoxy" and "heresy."[22]

On the theological level, we have seen that, according to several scholars, "orthodoxy" may well have been earlier and far more widespread than Bauer allowed (Davids, Heron, McCue, Norris, Simon). Part of the problem is that Bauer never adequately described the theology of orthodoxy and indeed seems not to have taken it very seriously. And there is still need to explore the theological significance of orthodoxy's eventual triumph (Chapman, Elze, Flora, Hawkin). Bauer's own description ("a curious quirk of history") is hardly adequate.

[22]See my article, "Sociological Concepts and the Early Church: A Decade of Research," *TS* 41 (1980) 181-90; see also R. Scroggs, "The Sociological Interpretation of the New Testament: The Present State of Research," *NTS* 26 (1979-80) 164-79.

11. THE ECUMENICAL IMPORTANCE OF NEW TESTAMENT RESEARCH

That eminent church historian and observer of the religious scene, Martin Marty, has recently called attention to the phenomenon of the "public church." The term refers to the symbiotic relationship that has developed among Catholics, mainline Protestants, and evangelicals in recent years. Working in the context of biblical witness, the public church promotes a realism about limits along with a limitless dream. It is committed to the public sector and to civility in dialogue. Its rivals are totalism, tribalism, and privatism.

On reading Marty's *The Public Church* (1981), one may wonder whether this church is a reality or merely the dream of a clever professor. But one area in which the public church most certainly is a reality is the field of New Testament research. There Catholics, mainline Protestants, evangelicals, and others use a common language and common methods to talk about the foundational documents of Christian faith. There scholars engage in what has developed into an interconfessional and international dialogue. There, at least, Professor Marty's public church is a living reality.

The Language of New Testament Study

Those who engage in ecumenical dialogue often speak about the "language problem" that they encounter. To outsiders the ecumenists' problems may sound excessively theoretical and even appear to be a delaying tactic designed to put off the more practical and pressing concerns of ecumenism. Yet the language problem in ecumenism is real. Catholics and Protestants have used terms in different ways, so that sometimes the words may be the same but the meanings differ. More commonly, the religious groups have constructed their own technical vocabularies in the light of various historical and philosophical developments. What appears to be a perfectly clear and coherent system of discourse to German Lutherans, may be foreign and forbidding to American Catholics. The initial task of serious ecumenical conversation is to understand the other person's language, to recognize the distinctive ways in which terms are used, to get beneath the surface to the deep structures of thought, to crack the code used by the partners in dialogue.

The language problem of ecumenism will not be solved quickly. Just as humility and patience are required to learn the language of another people, and just as in learning languages there is a rhythm of progress and regress, so ecumenical understanding is necessarily marked by slow and sometimes fitful development. If we are serious about the task of ecumenism and grasp the complexity of that task in even a rudimentary way, we cannot expect it to be otherwise. There is, however, a field of theological study in which the humility and patience demanded of participants in ecumenical conversation has already paid handsome dividends. It is New Testament research.

The ecumenical progress in New Testament research is a surprising and hopeful sign. It is a surprising sign because almost all Christian groups base their distinctive tenets and practices on the New Testament. Throughout the centuries, each Christian group has appealed to the text of the New Testament to explain itself and to suggest that all other groups have somehow deviated from the true faith taught by Jesus and the apostles. The surprise is that what had been the occasion of division in the past—the New Testament— has become an instrument of understanding and unity. It is a hopeful sign because if representatives of the various religious traditions can talk to one another about the New Testament, perhaps they can also talk humbly and patiently about other theological, historical, and pastoral issues.

The achievements of the biblical scholars in developing a common language and in understanding one another's views should give all church people encouragement and hope. Through contemporary New Testament research, the wish that "all may be one" is a little closer to being a reality.

What is the common language used in the New Testament research? It is basically the set of questions and concerns that has developed from centuries of interpreting written texts. The fundamental task of biblical study is to understand what the documents meant in their original historical setting, and so exegetes try to explain what the biblical writer communicated to the people of his time. Although a theoretical objection can be made against ever fully grasping the intention of any author (the so-called intentional fallacy), we can at least come close to understanding what a document meant in its original historical setting. The alternative is to let texts mean whatever we want them to mean, to use them as vehicles for our projections and prejudices, and to renounce the very possibility of communication across the boundaries of time and space.

How do exegetes go about establishing what the New Testament writings meant in their historical settings? Since the building blocks of all discourse are words and concepts, New Testament specialists seek to understand the meaning of terms in the ancient world and in the individual books of the Bible. All the New Testament books were written in Greek in the second half of the first century A.D. (with perhaps a few books even reaching into the second century).

Therefore all Greek writings from this time must be examined carefully in the hope of understanding how this word or that concept is used in the New Testament. Special attention is given to the Greek translation of the Old Testament (the Septuagint) and the writings of the common people (letters, business documents, legal documents, etc., in Koine Greek). The reason for this is obvious. The books of the New Testament were written almost entirely by Greek-speaking Jews, who were familiar with the Old Testament in its Greek translation. These books were also largely written by and for the common people of the Greco-Roman world, not for an intellectual elite. So the initial task of New Testament interpretation is to understand how a particular word or concept is used in a passage, how it figures in the biblical writer's total vision, and how this use compares with contemporary usage.

Words and concepts must also be studied as parts in a larger literary whole. If we are to understand the ideas of the New Testament writings, we must read them in their literary context. Enter the traditional concerns of literary criticism! Those who specialize in the literary criticism of the New Testament attend to the grammatical and syntactical relationships between the ideas and the terms. When a narrative is examined, attention is given to the characters: Who is the focus of attention? How do the other characters relate to the main character? What progress takes place in the story?

A very important concern of New Testament exegesis is the literary form of the large unit in which the words and concepts are used as parts. The genres or large forms of the New Testament are Gospel (the story of Jesus), Acts (the story of the early church's spread from Jerusalem to Rome), Epistle (letters from an apostle to one or several churches), and Apocalypse (a revelation of the past, present, and future). Within these genres is a dizzying variety of smaller literary forms such as genealogy, parable, miracle story, proverb, discourse, benediction, hymn, thanksgiving, confession of faith, homily, and vision.

The very multiplicity of literary forms suggests something very important about the New Testament books. They arose in a milieu in which originality and literary creativity were not the high values that they are today. They are deeply traditional works, incorporating ideas and even small units already current in early Christian circles. Those who wish to do justice to the nature of the New Testament writings must consider where this or that idea stands in the history of the tradition (tradition history), how and where the small units circulated in early Christianity (form history), what sources the writer used (source criticism), and how the traditional materials fit into the final form of the book composed by the author (redaction criticism). For fuller discussions of the theory and practice of contemporary biblical research, see my books, *Interpreting the New Testament* (1980) and *Interpreting the Old Testament* (1981), published by Michael Glazier of Wilmington, DE.

The Agenda for the Dialogue

The fact that almost all biblical scholars use the same basic language and methods creates the possibility of dialogue. But what gets discussed in the dialogue, and who sets the agenda? In this respect, New Testament research functions in much the same ways as other scholarly disciplines do. New discoveries are greeted with enthusiasm and subjected to careful examination. Old problems are reviewed in the light of the new discoveries and changing experience.

The past decade saw the publication of important materials from ancient times. The Dead Sea scrolls continue to appear at a slow pace, but the 1970's did witness the publication of the Targum of Job (an Aramaic paraphrase of the Hebrew book of Job), the Books of Enoch (the Aramaic originals of a corpus of apocalyptic writings), and the Temple Scroll (a verbal blueprint of the temple and related areas). The gnostic writings discovered at Nag Hammadi in Egypt have been made available in photographs and an English translation by James M. Robinson and a team of researchers. Those documents are important witnesses to the existence of gnostic currents in early Christian circles and may even shed light on Paul's spiritual rivals in the Mediterranean world of the first century. Archaeologists working in Israel have learned a good deal about synagogues, burial customs, and other social realities of Jesus' time. Of course, the most exciting discovery (in northeastern Jerusalem) was the skeleton of a man who had been crucified by being nailed to a cross. Careful examination of his bones has allowed a plausible reconstruction to be made of the procedures used in the crucifixion of Jesus.

New discoveries naturally occupy a high place on the agenda of biblical research. Unfortunate experiences in the past have taught biblical specialists to be cautious about their claims and to insist on the careful study of the evidence. Now that these important Dead Sea scrolls and the Nag Hammadi documents have been made public in a competent way, the comparisons with the New Testament can begin.

New Testament has not been the only discipline to profit from the new discoveries. The finding of the Dead Sea scrolls in the late 1940's has inspired the reexamination of all Jewish literature roughly contemporaneous with the New Testament: the Pseudepigrapha (extracanonical Jewish writings), Josephus (the Jewish historian) and Philo (the Alexandrian philosopher-exegete), the Targums (Aramaic paraphrases of the Old Testament), and other rabbinic writings. The discovery of the Nag Hammadi library in the late 1940's has also prompted a serious review of what the Fathers of the Church had said about gnosticism and how the church developed in the first four centuries. The archaeological finds in Israel have given us a window onto a much more diverse and exotic world of Judaism than was thought possible fifty years ago.

New Testament researchers neither sit around waiting for new discoveries, nor do they exist in a cultural vacuum. Besides the new discoveries and the reassessments inspired by them, the agenda of New Testament research is influenced by new looks at old theological problems, the issues facing the church today, cultural concerns, and concepts and methods taken from other fields.

Theological problems do not disappear, and theologians are always going back over old problems and coming away with new and clearer perceptions. New Testament theologians are mainly concerned with understanding and clarifying the theological thoughts of the biblical writers. This modest task can sometimes have dramatic effects for the whole of theology. For example, twenty years ago Krister Stendahl suggested that Paul did not have the "introspective conscience" attributed to him by Augustine and Luther and that the apostle was really interested in the socioreligious problem of how Gentiles could be members of God's people. The correctness of this insight is confirmed by the recent observation of another scholar that in fact no one in Paul's time had an introspective conscience and that everyone thought in terms of relationships with persons and groups. This approach to the context of Paul's theology demands the rethinking of the doctrine of justification in particular and of Western theology in general.

The setting for much New Testament study is the church, and so it is no surprise that the problems facing the church as an institution today occupy a prominent place on the agenda. Perhaps the most significant and pervasive contribution of New Testament research in this area has been the recognition and appreciation of the theological and cultural diversity within early Christianity. Each New Testament author had particular ways of looking at Christ, the world, and the church. There were different patterns of organization and even rival groups within the same community. The fact of early Christian theological and institutional diversity can liberate twentieth-century Christians from supposing that Christian unity must mean uniformity. It can also encourage church people as they deal with hard issues today (the structures of the church, the meaning of ministry, the ordination of women, etc.) to be creative in their solutions.

The agenda of New Testament study is also enlivened by contact with the culture in which it takes place. The late

1960's were surely a time of cultural crisis in North America and Western Europe. Apparently strong institutions and even governments suddenly seemed to be all too fragile. There is surely some connection between the cultural crisis of the late 1960's and the fascination with apocalypticism and with the resurrection of Jesus that was so prominent in biblical studies at the time. Likewise, the great concerns with violence and death during the 1970's certainly had an impact on the widespread interest shown by biblical specialists in Jesus' attitude toward violence and his understanding of his own death.

Other academic disciplines also contribute to the agenda for biblical research. By now the gains for biblical studies from secular historiography and archaeology are so obvious and well known that it is impossible to think of New Testament research without those related disciplines. But the past decade saw the arrival of some new partners in the dialogue. Concepts taken from sociology, cultural anthropology, and psychology have infused new life into old texts and have enabled us to understand in part why the New Testament is such a powerful collection of writings. The revolutions taking place in linguistics, structuralism, semantics, semiotics, and hermeneutics have made New Testament scholars reflect on the adequacy of their traditional philological and historical approaches. Electronic computers have been used in producing concordances, trying to resolve disputes about authorship, and organizing the materials discovered by archaeologists. Whether they like it or not, New Testament specialists have to add some new words, ideas, and methods to the languages that they have learned to talk to each other.

An Interconfessional and International Dialogue

It is sometimes said that "we can no longer speak of Catholic biblical study." That statement may be disturbing. It is also false if it denies the need for committed Catholic exegetes or the existence of problems peculiar to the Catholic tradition that need to be addressed in the light of

Scripture. But the statement is true in the sense that the biblical study done by Catholic exegetes is now part of a larger interconfessional and international dialogue. That dialogue has been made possible by the language of New Testament exegesis and is being enriched by the many religious and ethnic accents in which the language is spoken.

A most significant development toward full Catholic participation in this dialogue was made in 1965 by a statement in Vatican II's Constitution on Divine Revelation: "The interpreter must investigate what meaning the sacred writer intended to express and actually expressed in particular circumstances as he used contemporary literary forms in accordance with the situation of his own time and culture. For the correct understanding of what the sacred author wanted to assert, due attention must be paid to the customary and characteristic styles of perceiving, speaking, and narrating which prevailed at the time of the sacred writer, and to the customs people followed at that period in their everyday dealing with one another." I know no better summary of the task of biblical research than those words from Vatican II, and I know very few biblical scholars who would disagree with them. Of course, those two sentences are not the whole document. Nevertheless, they do encapsulate what the biblical scholars are trying to do and represent official church approval of their efforts.

The ecumenical significance of the language of New Testament study should not be underestimated. It made it possible for Catholic, Lutheran, and other Protestant exegetes to produce the balanced and valuable volumes, *Peter in the New Testament* (1974) and *Mary in the New Testament* (1978). It made it possible for me as a Jesuit professor of New Testament at the Weston School of Theology in Cambridge, MA, for the past ten years to join with my colleagues from Harvard Divinity School and Episcopal Divinity School in working out an annual slate of courses and in introducing students from the three schools to the content of the New Testament and the methods most appropriate for understanding it. It made it possible for the

New Testament professors from the nine theological schools in the Boston area to gather monthly for ten years to hear and discuss the results of one another's research.

The agenda of New Testament research is handled not only in such local forums but also in national and international meetings and in scholarly journals. The annual meetings of the Catholic Biblical Association have been greatly enriched for more than a decade by the active participation of Protestant scholars, and the much larger Society of Biblical Literature has routinely benefited from the editorial and organizational skills of Catholic scholars. The international Society of New Testament Studies gathers annually the most prominent Catholic and Protestant biblical scholars from all over the world.

The scholarly journals in the New Testament field—*New Testament Studies, Novum Testamentum, Biblica, Catholic Biblical Quarterly, Journal of Biblical Literature*—are open to all. The common language and methods are assumed, and the only requirement for publication is competency as judged by the editors. Few biblical scholars even give a second thought to what might astound outside observers: Catholics, mainline Protestants, evangelicals, Jews, and others publish the results of their biblical research in the same journals.

While there is one basic language in New Testament research, there are (happily) many accents. Some of those accents are old, but some are new. The common vocabulary and methods are presupposed, but there are factors in the intellectual traditions and the experiences of various nations that enable them to make unique contributions to the international dialogue.

Who can be unaware of the industry, analytical achievement, and intellectual power of German biblical scholarship? A special interest of German scholarship has been what was going on behind the texts: the conflicts, the opposing groups, the dialectic of ideas, etc. In countries like France, Italy, and Spain, where there is either a sharp division between the university and the church, or church control of the university, the traditional concerns of theology (Christology, miracles, ministry, the biblical foundations of popular piety, etc.) tend to dominate. The British continue the tradition of careful and conservative scholarship, with important contributions emanating from the evangelical tradition. North Americans have learned much from the Western Europeans, but their industry and organizational talents have made possible important gains in our understanding of the world in which the New Testament took shape. It would not be unfair to say that North America is now the center of New Testament research.

The international dialogue is now being enlivened by some new accents. Indian biblical scholars trained in the West are also trying to apply the traditional Indian methods of interpreting religious texts to the Bible and are exploring the extent to which the Indian religious tradition might serve as a preparation for the gospel. Latin American biblical scholars are reminding their fellows of the importance of group study of the Bible and calling attention to the political and ideological dimensions of much modern biblical scholarship. Israeli archaeologists are teaching us about the world in which Jesus and his first followers lived, and Jewish historians and theologians are reminding us persistently and eloquently about the Jewishness of Jesus. An African scholar from Tanzania concludes a competent review of the quest for the historical Jesus with a reminder that a Jesus robbed of all supernaturalism is meaningless to Africans. The feminist movement in the USA has led to good reexaminations of the place of women in earliest Christianity and to sophisticated reflections concerning what we do and do not know about the primitive church.

These few examples point to an important development in the world of religion. Men and women from different religious backgrounds and from all over the world are using a common language to talk about a single body of literature—the New Testament. They are enriching the ecumenical conversation in light of their intellectual traditions and their contemporary experiences.

What is being accomplished in New Testament research will not resolve all the problems that face Martin Marty's public church or even the Catholic church. Nor would I suggest for a moment that unanimity exists within the inter-confessional and international dialogue that takes place among New Testament scholars. But I do suggest that the acceptance of a common language (limited though it may be), the openness to new discoveries and to reexaminations of old questions, and the construction of channels for communication across denominational and national boundaries furnish a model for all who wish to further the cause of ecumenism.

12. SOME NEW VOICES IN NEW TESTAMENT INTERPRETATION

In recent years New Testament study has developed into an interconfessional and international dialogue. New Testament scholars have worked out a common language and methodology, revised previously accepted positions in the light of new evidence and further reflection, and constructed channels of communication across confessional and national boundaries.[1] This interconfessional and international dialogue is now being enlivened and enriched by some new voices emanating from nations and groups that had not previously been heard from.

The new voices come from India, Africa, Latin America, England, and the United States. They are chiefly concerned with the process of hermeneutics, and are challenging all New Testament scholars to greater clarity and honesty in biblical interpretation. They are doing so by making us more aware of the social settings in which we do biblical exegesis and theology, and by sensitizing us to the errors and unconscious prejudices that stand in the way of sound biblical exposition. These new voices are expressing them-

[1]D. J. Harrington, "The Ecumenical Importance of New Testament Research," *BTB* 12 (1982) 20-23.

selves mainly in articles published in periodicals with very limited circulations. The new voices deserve a wider hearing than they are getting from biblical specialists and theologians in North America and Europe.

India: Ashramites and Liberationists

A most articulate critic of the way that biblical exegesis is usually done in Western Europe and North America is the Indian Jesuit, George Soares-Prabhu.[2] His target is the so-called historical-critical method. His own doctoral dissertation, *The Formula Quotations in the Infancy Narrative of Matthew,* was published in the prestigious Analecta Biblica series and shows great skill in using the tools of modern historical criticism. But his experiences in teaching and pastoral work in India have led him to describe the historical-critical method as "ineffective, irrelevant, and ideologically loaded" (154) and to propose a distinctively Indian approach to biblical interpretation.

Since Soares-Prabhu's criticisms of the historical-critical method are echoed by many scholars from other lands, they are worth hearing out at this point. He judges the method ineffective, because it is not adequate for interpreting a religious text that deals with qualitative rather than quantitative realities and consists of words referring to experience-loaded, polyvalent realities. He judges it irrelevant, for its results seldom touch upon the concerns of ordinary people and are intelligible only to members of the guild of biblical scholars. He judges the method ideologically loaded, because it is so closely tied to Western European history. It was used originally by the Enlightenment to break the stranglehold of stagnant and reactionary ecclesiastical traditions that were stifling Europe's intellectual development and

[2]G. M. Soares-Prabhu, "Towards an Indian Interpretation of the Bible," *Biblebhashyam* 6 (1980) 151-70.

hindering its political growth. It continues to function (at least by default) as a legitimation of the capitalistic technocracy to which the Enlightenment led.

Soares-Prabhu admits that historical criticism cannot be by-passed. He simply doubts its sufficiency. Even though he describes the new hermeneutic, structuralism, rhetorical criticism, and the sociological and psychological approaches as flurried attempts to make the Bible relevant, he recognizes them at least as prospective partners in dialogue in developing an Indian approach to the Bible: "An Indian exegesis cannot be an exotic plant growing in isolation out of the humid soil of traditional Indian methods of interpretation. Rather it will result from the cross fertilization of modern methods of biblical interpretation with contributions from Indian exegetical tradition, coming to flower in the strong climate of the socio-cultural reality of India today" (167).

Relevance—in particular, the practical quest for liberation—has always been the goal of traditional Hindu theology, and so an Indian biblical exegesis will be greatly concerned with relevance. Two approaches are possible. The "ashramite" or religious approach will apply the traditional methods of Indian exegesis to the biblical text and transpose its Hebrew and Greek symbols into Indian ones. The aim, however, is not to discover traditional Indian values in the Bible. Rather, the task facing the ashramite is to find an Indian language for the specific incarnational insights of biblical religion; that is, humanity as the place of one's encounter with God, and the relation between love of God and love of neighbor.

The second possible approach is the "liberationist" or social one. This approach will try to read the Bible in the light of a liberating praxis among the socially oppressed, without succumbing to the sociological reductionism of a strictly Marxist orientation. The aim is not to find in the Bible the validation of a socioeconomic analysis. Rather, the task is to search the biblical text for transmaterial and anticonsumerist values that can inspire a change of attitude resulting in a genuine social revolution.

These two approaches correspond to the two major currents in Indian Christian theology today. The ashramites are pursuing a dialogue with traditional Indian religiosity, and the liberationists are working at the conscientization of the oppressed masses of the land. Soares-Prabhu hopes that the two currents can engender complementary methods of reading the Bible and will eventually converge on a dialectical center. He also feels that this development can have significance far beyond the borders of India.

Africa: A More Biblical View of the World

One easy way to become sensitive to black African discontent with the conventional historical-critical method is through S. O. Abogunrin's article, "The Modern Search of the Historical Jesus in Relation to Christianity in Africa."[3] As the title indicates, the bulk of the paper traces the fortunes of the quest for the historical Jesus during the nineteenth and twentieth centuries. Abogunrin distinguishes three major stages through which the quest has passed: the nineteenth-century historians' unsuccessful effort at reconstructing the biography of Jesus by use of a supposedly objective historical method, early twentieth-century attempts at relegating to the background the relevance of the Gospels' history for Christian faith, and more recent efforts at reestablishing the Jesus of history for Christian faith.

What makes Abogunrin's critical survey important for our purposes is his final section on the quest and Africa. He begins by asking: "Has the debate on the quest of the historical Jesus anything to say to Africa, if indeed it has anything to say to the West?" (25). In fact, the author goes on to consider what Africa can say to the West on this matter and makes some sharp points.

Abogunrin's first point is that the thought-world of Africa and the thought-world of the Bible are very close.

[3]S. O. Abogunrin, "The Modern Search of the Historical Jesus in Relation to Christianity in Africa," *Africa Theological Journal* 9/3 (1980) 18-29.

Therefore, African Christians have a natural advantage over Westerners in relating the Gospel stories to their own situation. The second point is best expressed in the author's own words: "A Jesus emptied of all supernaturalism that we know about him in the New Testament, a Jesus who is merely an ordinary man like any other man will be meaningless in the African context"(26). The third point is related to the first two: "The majority of Africans still live in the Bible-world where the belief in demons and a host of unseen spiritual powers are potent and real" (26). In such a world the idea of Jesus as the conqueror of demons and the destroyer of all the spiritual forces of evil is very powerful.

The closeness in world-views between the Bible and Africa today, the positive significance attributed to the supernatural elements in the Gospels, and the liveliness of belief in demons—all these points boil down to the recognition that Africans need not and should not replicate the intellectual history of Western Europe in order to understand what the Gospels say about Jesus.

Monsengwo Pasinya, professor of exegesis on the Catholic theological faculty at Kinshasa in Zaire, has long been interested in the history and theory of hermeneutics. His doctoral dissertation dealt with the notion of *nomos* in the Greek Pentateuch. His article on African interpretation of the Bible places the task in the context of hermeneutical theory from Origen to Paul Ricoeur.[4] In fact, he takes up some of Ricoeur's ideas and develops them with specific reference to African biblical interpretation. The fundamental point is that even in the constitution of the biblical text it is necessary to distinguish various hermeneutical moments. Furthermore, without the continuing process of interpretation the biblical text would not exist. Interpretation is never completed; it always has new moments. This hermeneutical perspective allows Monsengwo to conclude that an African interpretation of the biblical message is an application, consequence, and variant of existential interpretation.

---

[4]Monsengwo Pasinya, "Interprétation africaine de la Bible. Racine herméneutique biblique," *Revue Africaine de Théologie* 1 (1977) 145-64.

Monsengwo's article is perhaps more illuminating on reflection than it may appear on first reading. This is so, because the article places the stirrings toward a distinctively African interpretation of the Scriptures in a multidimensional context. First of all, it ties African interpretation in with the process of transmission and interpretation that was constitutive of the Hebrew Old Testament, the Greek Septuagint, and the New Testament. It also makes a connection with the entire history of Christian and Jewish biblical interpretation. African interpretation emerges as a new moment in a long tradition. Second, it relates the movement toward an African interpretation to the very sophisticated hermeneutical theory of Paul Ricoeur, thus defending the African undertaking against charges of sloganeering and intellectual naiveté. Finally, it locates the point at which most of the present-day discontent with the conventional historical-critical method arises—at the level of existential interpretation.

Few Third-World biblical scholars wish to disregard the progress made by Westerners in philology, literary criticism, and historical research during the past two-hundred years. Their major complaint is with those of us who give the impression that biblical interpretation can stop at this pseudo-objective level and fail to take into account the complexity and richness of textual interpretation. The African enterprise deserves our attention in the years to come.

Latin America: Texts for Liberation

The best entry into the concerns and contributions of Latin American biblical interpretation is by way of Rudolf Renfer's recent essay in *Bulletin du Centre Protestant des Etudes.*[5] A summary of that article will provide us with a map. Then we can take a closer look at three of the main roads.

---

[5]R. Renfer, "L'enjeu du message biblique en Amérique latine," *Bulletin du Centre Protestant des Etudes* 33/6-7 (1981) 7-42.

After quoting three documents concerning the so-called base communities in Latin America, Renfer treats praxis as the point of departure for biblical interpretation in Latin America and the exodus-event as the hermeneutical principle. Then he discusses Severino Croatto's interpretation of the Christ-event in light of the exodus-event, Juan-Luis Segundo's insistence that biblical interpretation implies the liberation of theology, the militant exegesis of Gustavo Gutiérrez and Alejandro Cussianovich, and José Míguez Bonino's theory of "engaged" reading of the Bible. He closes by asking whether the hermeneutic of liberation theology contains an ideological tendency and by describing Latin American theology (which is rooted in biblical interpretation) as "by the people, in the people, and for the people" (41).

The three major roads on this map are the life-setting of biblical exegesis, the exodus-event as the hermeneutical key to the Bible and to life today, and the construction of the hermeneutical circle.

What makes Latin American biblical interpretation so distinctive is its consciousness of its own life-setting. The primary life-setting is the base community, which first took shape in popular Catholicism. The base communities have shown a strong tendency toward social and political engagement and a special concern for the poor and oppressed of the continent. The sociological phenomenon of the base communities is the place out of which the most creative theological currents have emerged, even if they have been worked out in written form by seminary professors and other academicians. To members of the base communities, the social and political problems of Latin America are clear. In this context, the action of God witnessed in the Scriptures is seen as parallel to the present-day action of God among the peoples of Latin America. The Bible is read and practiced in a life-setting exposed to violence, repression, torture, and social conflicts. It is read and practiced in the light of today's experience. The Western European and North American concerns with demythologizing and respiritualizing are viewed as foreign and nonapplicable. The world of the Scriptures is seen to be very close to the world of Latin America today.

The present-day Latin American experience of oppression and dependency leads logically back to the biblical account of the exodus of Israel from Egypt. In this respect the Latin American theologians are only following what historical-critical exegetes have pointed to as the central tradition of the Old Testament. But they maintain that the social and political consequences of the exodus-tradition have not been taken seriously enough by Western European and North American theologians. The exodus from Egypt took place in history. The exodus gave focus to the various traditions in the Old Testament and provided the context for understanding the Christ-event in the New Testament. The Christ-event extends the good news of the exodus and gives new dimensions to the meaning of liberation. The actions, words, and life of Jesus Christ liberate human beings oppressed by social and religious structures and allow them to speak the prophetic word.

Despite their emphasis on the closeness between the world of the Bible and the world of Latin America, and on the central significance of the exodus-tradition in the Bible, the Latin American theologians are not fundamentalists. The present situation, not the past, is their starting-point. The exodus-tradition is constantly reinterpreted and reexperienced along the lines of the hermeneutical theory of Paul Ricoeur. The goal is the establishing of a hermeneutical circle between the biblical text and Latin American experience. In constructing this hermeneutical circle, Juan-Luis Segundo has distinguished four steps: (1) Our experience of reality leads us to an ideological suspicion ("something is wrong"); (2) the ideological suspicion is then applied to every ideological superstructure and to theology in particular; (3) this new experience of theological reality leads to an exegetical suspicion, a suspicion that current biblical interpretation does not take into consideration some hermeneutical points of great importance; (4) one arrives at a new way of interpreting the Bible as the source of our faith, with new elements at our disposition.

Challenges from Judaism and Feminism

The voices that we have heard up to this point have come from India, Africa, and Latin America—areas that we have become accustomed to call the Third World. These voices claim in various ways that people in their social and cultural settings not only have valuable contributions to make in interpreting Scripture but even hold a kind of privileged position in grasping what is truly important in Scripture for today. At this point I would like to call attention to two voices from the First World—Judaism and feminism—that raise questions about how adequate is our understanding of the world in which the early church and the New Testament arose.

Geza Vermes, professor of Jewish studies at Oxford, is respected and admired by Christian and Jewish scholars alike for his many contributions to our understanding of Judaism and early Christianity between 200 B.C. and A.D. 400. In his recent article on Jewish studies and New Testament interpretation, he somewhat uncharacteristically expresses his views on broad methodological matters.[6] His first major point is a summons to both Christians and Jews to recognize how negative their relationship has been from the late first century A.D. to 1945. The major modes of communication have been polemics and apologies. In those rare instances where learned Christians such as the seventeenth-century British scholar John Lightfoot and the German Lutheran pastor Paul Billerbeck used Jewish religious documents in interpreting the New Testament, there was still little sympathy or positive feeling for the Jewish material. But as Vermes observes: "Religious writings disclose their meaning only to those who approach them in a spirit of sympathy" (6).

[6]G. Vermes, "Jewish Studies and New Testament Interpretation," *JJS* 31 (1980) 1-17.

There have been, however, some positive developments since 1945. These are attributable to two main causes. The first cause is the impact on the Christian world of the horror of the Holocaust, which has made anti-Judaism, even in its more refined academic form, not only unfashionable but also obscene. The second cause is the discovery of the Dead Sea scrolls in the vicinity of Qumran between 1947 and 1956. These documents have both revived interest in the Jewish background of the New Testament and illumined the terms, concepts, and institutions of early Christianity. These two factors—the horror of the Holocaust, and the discovery of the Qumran scrolls—have contributed to the growing recognition that no adequate understanding of early Christian sources is conceivable without expertise in the Jewish background of the New Testament.

The phrase "Jewish background," however, is not as innocuous or neutral as it may initially sound. Too often, Vermes observes, the Jewish background is studied only for the help that it can offer in solving New Testament puzzles; it is allowed to speak only when spoken to. But for a truly historical understanding, the age-old distinction between the New Testament and its Jewish background should be abolished and the former looked at deliberately as a part of a larger whole. Furthermore, the character of the New Testament as a translation of Semitic terms and ideas into Greek must be more widely acknowledged. The revival of scholarship that Vermes and others hope for in both Christian and Jewish circles will not take place "until interpreters of the Christian Gospels learn to immerse themselves in the native religion of Jesus the *Jew,* and in the general climate of thought of the world and age in which he lived" (17).

Jewish scholars like Vermes are challenging Christians and Jews alike to recognize the sad character of their past relationship, the positive developments in recent years, and the need for further reflection on how Jewish and early Christian sources can be studied better. But Jewish scholars are not the only ones expressing dissatisfaction with our conventional understanding of early Christianity. In fact, Carolyn Osiek has compared the presence of misogynism in the Bible to the problem of anti-Semitism in the New Testament.[7] That comparison sounds harsh, but it does express the viewpoint of many women biblical scholars that not all is right with the way we are accustomed to think about early Christian history.

Articles by Bernadette Brooten[8] and Elizabeth Schüssler Fiorenza[9] have expressed very clearly the problems that feminists see in the commonly accepted reconstructions of early Christian life. Both contend that the evidence for the important contributions made by women in the Pauline mission and other phases in the spread of Christianity has been either ignored or misinterpreted. They also note that many of these contributions may well have been suppressed and are now irretrievable because the men who selected and edited the literary materials of early Christianity viewed the contributions made by women as unimportant or threatening.

Brooten contends that the influence of patriarchy extended even to the content of theological statements in early Christianity and that some writers tried to maintain the patriarchy by means of Old Testament and other theological arguments. But she rightly cautions against monolithic depictions of Jewish or Greco-Roman patriarchy that are created solely to make Christianity seem progressive by comparison. Schüssler Fiorenza recommends a return to the countercultural, egalitarian impulses of the Jesus movement and the early Christian mission. She feels that only this model can do justice to both the traditions of women's leadership in the early church and the gradual process of adaptation and theological justification of the dominant patriarchal Greco-Roman culture and society.

[7] C. Osiek, "Inspired Texts: The Dilemma of the Feminist Believer," *Spirituality Today* 32 (1980) 138-47.

[8] B. Brooten, "Feminist Perspectives on New Testament Exegesis," *Concilium* 138 (1980) 55-61.

[9] E. Schussler Fiorenza, " 'You are not to be called Father.' Early Christian History in a Feminist Perspective," *Cross Currents* 29 (1979) 301-23.

Conclusion

We have tried to listen to some new voices in the interconfessional and international dialogue that is New Testament interpretation today. From Soares-Prabhu, we have heard some sharp criticisms of the conventional way of interpreting the Bible and some good suggestions about the religious and social possibilities of a distinctively Indian approach. Abogunrin has reminded us that Africans can enter the world of the Bible more easily than Westerners can, and Monsengwo Pasinya has shown that the African interpretation of the Bible is a new moment in a long tradition and rests on solid hermeneutical foundations. The Latin American biblical theologians have made us more conscious of the life-setting of biblical study, the central significance of the exodus, and the hermeneutical circle between present-day experience and the biblical text. Vermes has given us suggestions on how Jewish sources can be used more effectively in New Testament study, and Brooten and Schüssler Fiorenza have indicated how different early Christianity can look when viewed from the feminist perspective.

INDEX OF MODERN SCHOLARS

Abel, E.L., 99, 152
Abogunrin, S.O., 189-90, 197
Aland, K., 39
Appel, N., 37-38
Arndt, W.F., 123

Bacon, B.W., 97-98, 109
Banks, R., 108
Barbour, R.S., 31
Barth, G., 94
Barth, K., 34-35
Bartlett, D.L., 153
Barton, D.M., 93
Batey, R., 31
Bauer, W., 13, 78, 123, 162-73
Becker, J., 118
Behm, J., 71
Bell, D., 156
Berger, K., 150
Bertram, G., 111
Billerbeck, P., 194
Blair, E.P., 106
Bloch, E., 40
Boismard, M.-E., 95
Bornkamm, G., 31, 94-95
Bouttier, M., 42
Brooten, B., 196-97
Brown, R.E., 39, 41-42
Brown, S., 149
Bruner, F.D., 47-60
Bultmann, R., 15, 22, 34-36, 70, 160
Burger, C., 96
Burgess, J.A., 142

Cahill, P.J., 31
Carlston, C.E., 95
Chapman, G.C., 39-40, 169, 173
Charles, R.H., 118
Clark, K.W., 111, 116
Comber, J.A., 123
Congar, Y., 39
Conzelmann, H., 34, 64, 68, 142
Cope, L., 119, 123
Cothenet, E., 101
Croatto, S., 192
Cussianovich, A., 192

Davids, A., 168, 173
Davies, W.D., 100, 119, 157
de Jonge, M., 118
Derrett, J.D.M., 96
Dibelius, M., 142
Didier, M., 97
Dodd, C.H., 87-88
Donahue, J.R., 139
Downing, F.G., 31
Drijvers, H.J.W., 172
Dunn, J.D.G., 47-60, 170-72

Elliott, J.H., 63, 77, 158
Ellis, E.E., 164
Elze, M., 167, 173

Farmer, W.R., 95
Feine, P., 71
Ferrar, W.F., 122
Fiedler, M.J., 94

Fisher, E.J., 144
Flora, J.R., 166, 169-70, 173
Frankemölle, H., 103, 111
Frend, W.H.C., 165
Fuchs, A., 95
Fuchs, E., 21
Fuller, R.H., 95

Gaboury, A., 95
Gager, J.G., 149, 151-55
Gaston, L., 106
Gerhardsson, B., 105
Gibbs, J.M., 106
Gingrich, F.W., 123
Gnilka, J., 71
Gogarten, F., 34-35
Goulder, M.D., 94, 96
Grant, R.M., 149
Green, H.B., 97
Griesbach, J.J., 95
Gundry, R.H., 107
Gutiérrez, G., 192

Haible, E., 42
Hamerton-Kelly, R.G., 108
Hare, D.R.A., 12, 100, 111, 120, 123
Harrington, D.J., 143, 164, 186
Hartman, L., 107
Hasenhüttl, G., 43
Hasler, V., 94
Hawkin, D.J., 169, 173
Held, H.J., 94
Heron, A.I.C., 166, 173
Hill, D., 94, 102
Hubbard, B.J., 105, 117
Hummel, R., 94

Isenberg, S., 156

Jackson, H., 152
Jeremias, J., 119
Johnson, M.D., 106
Johnston, G., 164
Jülicher, A., 34-35

Käsemann, E., 9-12, 15-45, 61-62, 76
Kelly, J.N.D., 73
Kilpatrick, G.D., 121

Kingsbury, J.D., 98-99, 104-105, 123
Kippenberg, H.G., 154
Knox, J., 78
Koester, H., 170, 172
Kraabel, A.T., 164, 172
Kraft, R.A., 163, 170
Kretzer, A., 103
Krodel, G., 163
Kümmel, W.G., 71
Küng, H., 31, 38, 42-44, 76, 148

Lange, J., 105, 116
Légasse, S., 100
Léon-Dufour, X., 95
Lightfoot, J., 194
Lohfink, G., 138
Lohse, E., 71
Longenecker, R.N., 164
Longstaff, T.R.W., 95
Luz, U., 101

Malherbe, A.J., 149
Malina, B.J., 155-56
Markus, R.A., 165
Marshall, I.H., 166, 172
Martin, B.L., 166
Martin, J.P., 103
Marty, M., 174, 185
McConnell, R.S., 107
McCue, J.F., 168, 173
McDonnell, K., 44
McHugh, J., 165
McMillon, L.A., 164
Meeks, W.A., 157
Meier, J.P., 105, 123
Meschke, K., 98
Metzger, B.M., 67
Míguez Bonino, J., 192
Minear, P.S., 41, 102
Mitton, C.L., 71
Moltmann, J., 40
Monsengwo Pasinya, L., 190-91, 197
Moriarty, F.L., 12
Murphy, C., 164

Neufeld, K.H., 62
Neusner, J., 156

Niebuhr, H.R., 44
Nineham, D., 150
Norris, F.W., 168, 173

O'Connor, E.D., 46
O'Neill, J.C., 34
Osborn, E., 6
Osborne, R.E., 100
Osiek, C., 195-96

Pagels, E., 171-72
Pesch, W., 99
Peterson, E., 15, 36
Punge, M., 94

Rabin, B., 112
Rabin, C., 112
Rackham, H., 123
Rader, W., 146
Rahner, K., 43, 142
Ramaroson, L., 98
Reese, J.M., 123
Renfer, R., 191-92
Reumann, J., 31
Ricoeur, P., 190-91
Robinson, J.M., 31, 34, 95, 170, 178
Rohde, J., 93-94, 109
Rolland, P., 97
Rothfuchs, W., 107
Ryan, T.J., 157

Said, E., 149
Sand, A., 108-09
Sanders, E.P., 95
Sandmel, S., 144
Schild, M., 164
Schillebeeckx, E., 44
Schlatter, A., 15
Schmidt, K.L., 111
Schnackenburg, R., 41
Schoedel, W.R., 167
Scholem, G., 156
Schreiber, A., 158
Schüssler Fiorenza, E., 196-97
Schütz, J.H., 159
Schweizer, E., 94, 99, 101
Scroggs, R., 157, 173
Segundo, J.-L., 192-93
Senior, D., 97
Sheridan, M., 101

Shils, E., 159
Simon, M., 167, 173
Simonsen, H., 108
Simpson, R.T., 96
Sloyan, G.S., 139
Smith, J.Z., 153
Soares-Prabhu, G., 187-89, 197
Songer, H.O., 169
Stead, G.C., 165
Stein, R.H., 95
Stendahl, K., 108, 144, 180
Stevenson, E., 150
Strecker, G., 94, 104, 163, 165, 170
Suggs, M.J., 106
Suhl, A., 106

Tagawa, K., 100
Theissen, G., 149-51, 154-55, 158
Thompson, W.G., 94, 96-97, 99, 104, 123
Thysman, R., 103
Tracy, D., 154
Trilling, W., 94, 102, 117-20
Troeltsch, E., 78
Turner, H.E.W., 169

van den Broek, R., 167, 172
Van Segbroeck, F., 107
van Tilborg, S., 99, 102
Vawter, B., 164
Vermes, G., 194-95, 197
Vielhauer, P., 66
von Campenhausen, H., 38, 70
von Harnack, A., 34-35

Walker, R., 104, 111
Walker, W.O., 103
Ward, M., 165
Weber, M., 153, 159, 173
Weiss, B., 111
Weiss, J., 34
Wernik, U., 152
West, H.P., 96
Wilckens, U., 34
Wilken, R.L., 167
Wilkins, W., 96
Williams, D.D., 44
Williams, R.B., 152
Woolley, P., 164
Worgul, G.S., 156

67126

Wrege, H.-T., 96

Yadin, Y., 112

Zahn, T., 120
Zahrnt, H., 31, 34

DATE DUE

NOV 20 '85			
DEC 14 '88			
MAY 10 '89			

DEMCO 38-297